CAROL VORDE[RMAN]
Maths Made Eas[y]

10 Minutes A Day
Problem Solving

Ages 7-9

Authors
Sean McArdle and Darius McArdle

Consultant
Sean McArdle

This timer counts up to 10 minutes.
When it reaches 10:00 it will beep.

How to use the timer:
Switch the timer ON.
Press the triangle ▶ to START the timer.
Press the square ■ to STOP or PAUSE the timer.
Press the square ■ to RESET the timer to 00:00.
Press any button to WAKE UP the timer.

Contents

Editors Jolyon Goddard, Nishtha Kapil
Art Editor Dheeraj Arora
Managing Editor Soma B. Chowdhury
Managing Art Editors Richard Czapnik, Ahlawat Gunjan
Art Director Martin Wilson
Senior Producer, Pre-Production Ben Marcus
Producer Christine Ni
Maths Consultant Sean McArdle
DTP Designer Anita Yadav

First published in Great Britain in 2015 by
Dorling Kindersley Limited
80 Strand, London, WC2R 0RL

Copyright © 2015 Dorling Kindersley Limited
A Penguin Random House Company
10 9 8 7 6 5
006–270405–July/2015

All rights reserved.
No part of this publication may be reproduced, stored in or introduced into a retrieval system, or transmitted, in any form, or by any means (electronic, mechanical, photocopying, recording, or otherwise), without the prior written permission of the copyright owner.

A CIP catalogue record for this book
is available from the British Library.
ISBN: 978-0-2411-8386-1

Printed and bound in China

All images © Dorling Kindersley Limited
For further information see: www.dkimages.com

A WORLD OF IDEAS:
SEE ALL THERE IS TO KNOW

www.dk.com

 Time taken

- **4** Seconds, minutes and hours
- **6** Days, weeks and months
- **8** Years, decades and centuries
- **10** The 24-hour clock
- **12** More time problems
- **14** Money problems 1
- **16** Length problems 1
- **18** Length problems 2
- **20** Perimeter problems
- **22** Areas of squares and rectangles

Time filler:
In these boxes are some extra challenges to extend your skills. You can do them if you have some time left after finishing the questions and continue until you hear the 10-minute beep. Or, these can be stand-alone activities that you can do in 10 minutes.

24	Areas of compound shapes	46	Addition and subtraction 2
26	Weights and measures 1	48	Multiplication and division 1
28	Weights and measures 2	50	Multiplication and division 2
30	Money problems 2	52	Money problems 3
32	Decimals 1	54	Times tables problems 1
34	Decimals 2	56	Times tables problems 2
36	Fractions	58	Ratio problems 1
38	Fractions and percentages	60	Ratio problems 2
40	Understanding graphs 1	62	Harder problems 1
42	Understanding graphs 2	64	Harder problems 2
44	Addition and subtraction 1	66	Parents' notes and answers

4 Seconds, minutes and hours

Knowing your times tables will help you convert between seconds, minutes and hours.

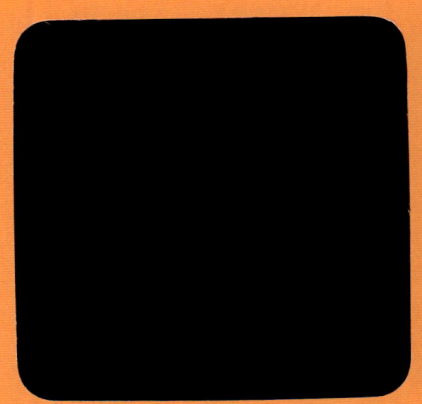

1) How many seconds are there in one hour?

2) How many minutes are there in one day?

3) Amir takes 20 minutes to walk to school and his sister Cala takes 25 minutes to walk the same distance. When their father takes them to school by car, the journey takes only six minutes. How much faster is the car journey for each child?

Amir gains   Cala gains

4) Sam takes 1 hour 50 minutes to walk home. It is five times quicker for him if he takes a bus home. How long will Sam take to reach home by bus?

Time filler:
Work out how much time you spend each day watching TV, doing homework, playing computer games and eating. Work out the time in hours and minutes first and then just in minutes.

(5) Add together the number of minutes in one hour, three-quarters of an hour, half an hour and a quarter of an hour.

(6) Terry likes his eggs to be boiled for 270 seconds. How long is that in minutes and seconds?

(7) Henri and Françoise play a computer game and use a timer to record their time taken. Henri completes the game in 2 minutes 38 seconds and Françoise completes it in 1 minute 42 seconds. How much quicker is Françoise than Henri?

(8) It takes Dani 3 hours 45 minutes to complete the first ten levels of a new game. Alexander, however, completes them in only 55 minutes. How much quicker was Alexander than Dani?

6

Days, weeks and months

Converting quickly between days and weeks helps you practise your seven times table.

1. Daisy's grandmother gives her 50 p every week as pocket money. If Daisy has collected £4 without spending any money, for how many months has she been getting money from her grandmother?

    ☐ months

2. Mario takes four days to travel to a holiday resort with his parents. He stays at the resort for 11 days and returns home by a different route, which takes only two days. How long is the whole trip in weeks and days?

   ☐ weeks ☐ days

3. Bogdan wants to travel the world and begins by spending 12 weeks in Poland. He then spends 24 weeks in the United States, eight weeks in Australia and 12 weeks in China. Lastly, he spends four weeks in South Africa before returning home. How long does Bogdan spend travelling? Write your answer in months.

   ☐ months

4. Add together the number of days in the months of May, June and July.

   ☐ days

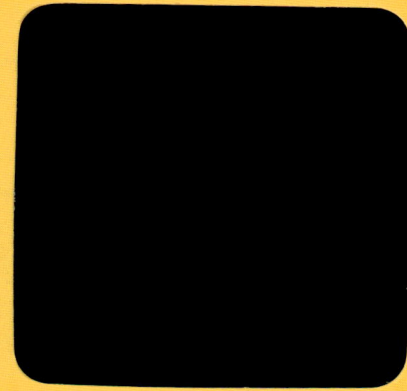

Time filler:
Write down the birthdays of your family members. Work out the gaps between the dates in:
- months, weeks and days
- weeks and days
- days.

5 List the months that have 30 days, the months that have 31 days and the month that usually has 28 days.

Months with 30 days ....

Months with 31 days ....

The month with 28 days usually ....

6 Bella has tests coming up in four weeks' time. She decides to revise five days each week and take the remaining days of the week off. How many days will Bella spend doing her revision?

☐ days

7 How many months are there in 12 years?

☐ months

8 A sailor has been on a ship for 60 days. How many weeks and days is that?

☐ weeks ☐ days

Years, decades and centuries

How quickly and accurately can you answer these questions?

1) A crack in a wall widens by about 1 cm each year. If the crack is 3 cm wide now, how wide will it be after…

   1 year? ☐   1 decade? ☐

2) Jacob was born in 2004.

   How old will Jacob be in the year 2017? ☐ years

   In which decade will Jacob be 50? ☐

3) Here is a list of some famous events in British history. Look at the years in which they happened. Write the year a century before and a century after each event.

Event	Year	Century before	Century after
Battle of Hastings	1066		
Great Fire of London	1666		
Beginning of World War I	1914		

Time filler:
Find out the years your grandparents, parents, uncles and aunts were born in. Now work out how much older than you they are in years and decades.

④ What is the year a decade before each of these years?

    2008   1990   2003

⑤ What is the year a decade after each of these years?

    1972   1995   2015

⑥ What is the year a century before each of these years?

    1918   1999   2015

⑦ What is the year a century after each of these years?

    980   1999   1968

⑧ What name do we give to a period of 1000 years?

The 24-hour clock

10

Test your understanding of the 24-hour system. Have a great time!

---

1) Mary wants to eat a meal at 17:30. It will take 45 minutes for the meal to cook. At what time should Mary's mother put the meal in the oven? Write your answer in the 24-hour format.

---

2) A film begins at 7.30 p.m. and is 2 hours 35 minutes long. At what time does the film end? Write your answer in the 24-hour format.

---

3) Lunchtime at a school begins at 12:30 and ends at 13:10. How long is lunchtime?

---

4) Hector plans to see some friends. The bus timetable shows time using the 24-hour system, which Hector does not understand. Hector's bus leaves at 09:15 and reaches his destination at 10:05. To return home, Hector must take the 16:20 bus that will get him back at 17:10.

To help Hector, change each of these 24-hour times to 12-hour times.

09:15   10:05

16:20   17:10

Time filler:
Make a chart showing which time system the devices in your home display. List the devices under these headings: **24-hour system**; **12-hour system**; and **Either**, for devices that can be changed from one system to the other.

5) A football match begins at 14:00 and lasts for 1 hour 47 minutes. At what time does the match end? Write your answer in the 24-hour format.

6) Write the following times in the 24-hour system:

Five minutes before noon

Five minutes after noon

7) How many minutes are there between 23:10 and 00:05?

8) Pam and Zoe have a ballet class at 15:20 and spend 1 hour 10 minutes there. At what time does the class end? Write your answer in the 12-hour format.

More time problems

Always be careful when changing between units.

1) Two teachers recorded the time taken by children in a race. One teacher recorded the time in minutes and seconds and the other recorded it in seconds. The table below shows the results.

Name	Time taken
Stuart	2 minutes 5 seconds
Li	120 seconds
Mona	172 seconds
Zan	1 minute 55 seconds

Look at the results and find out who won the race.

How much longer did Stuart take than Li?

2) Sophie and Jake have to travel from London to Birmingham. The journey should take about 2 hours 10 minutes. If Sophie and Jake leave London at 11.35 a.m., what time will they arrive in Birmingham?

3) What is 50 hours in days and hours?

4) A snail took eight hours to travel 1 m. How long did the snail take to travel each 10 cm?

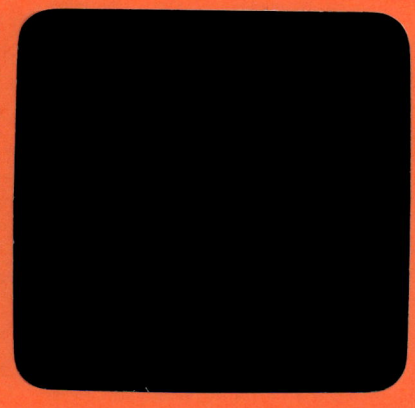

Time filler:
Can you work out using a calculator how many seconds there are in a year?
Hint: use 365 as the number of days in a year.

⑤ A train left Winchester at 10:03. Before reaching London Waterloo, the train waited at a signal for eight minutes. It arrived at London Waterloo at 11:05. If the train had not stopped at the signal, how long would the journey have taken?

⑥ How many hours are the same as 300 minutes?

⑦ Which is longer: 170 seconds or 2 minutes 40 seconds?

⑧ Darius and Emma have a 10-week holiday between leaving college and going to university. Their holiday begins in the first week of July.

In which month will their holiday end?

In which month will they be halfway through their holiday?

Money problems 1

Whenever you spend some cash, always make sure you receive the correct change.

1. Ben's mum uses a £10 voucher to download six books from a website. Each book costs 89p. How much money will she have left after buying the six books?

2. Pam likes to play an online game that costs her 40p per hour. If she plays the game for 29 hours in a month, how much will it cost her?

3. Emmie likes a winter coat she saw at a store for £67.99. She will get a discount of £12.50 if she buys the coat online. How much will the coat cost online?

4. Half of an amount is 85p. How much is the whole amount?

5. A magazine costs £3.50. During a special sale, it was sold at half its price. How much was the magazine sold for?

Time filler:
Using a maximum of five coins, come up with different ways to make a total of £1. One way, for example, is two 50 p coins .

⑥ How much is 35 p less than £5?

⑦ A one-way train ticket costs £3.60 and a return ticket for the same journey costs £4.20. If a lady buys two one-way tickets instead of a return ticket, how much extra will the tickets cost her?

⑧ Fran and Joseph went to a carnival together. They spent £2 on tickets, £1.60 on balloons, 70 p on candy floss and 80 p on masks. If they started with a total amount of £10 between them, how much money do they have left?

⑨ Danny was given £20 for his birthday to treat his friends. Following advice from his mum, Danny saved a quarter of the money for himself. How much money was Danny left with?

Length problems 1

It is important to know all the units used to measure length and their abbreviations.

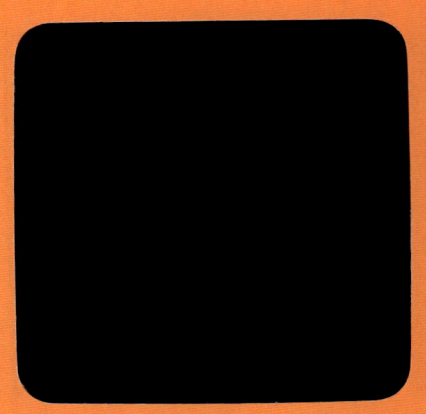

1. John has a model racetrack that is 3 m long. During the school holidays, John plans to double its length. How long will the new track be?

2. Gary's father covers 10 laps of a running track every day for one week. The track is 0.4 km long. What distance does Gary's father run in one week?

3. Convert each of these lengths into millimetres.

   2.5 m   3.1 m   0.075 m

4. A mile is about 1.6 km. How far would 5 miles be in kilometres?

Time filler:
Measure the height of each person in your family and then work out the differences between each of their heights.

5) How many centimetres are equal to 1 km?

6) Add these lengths and write the answer in millimetres.

2.5 cm + 12 mm + 3.4 cm

7) Anne's parents measure her height on her birthday every year. On her sixth birthday, Anne was 111 cm tall and by her seventh birthday she was 9 cm taller. On her eighth birthday, she had grown another 10 cm. How tall was Anne on her eighth birthday?

8) Write these distances in metres.

2.5 km   160 cm   31 km

Length problems 2

Here's some more practice in measuring lengths and changing between units.

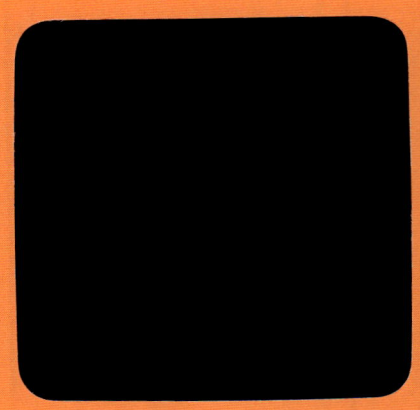

(1) A garden hedge that is 27 m long is being trimmed. Half of the hedge has already been trimmed. What length remains?

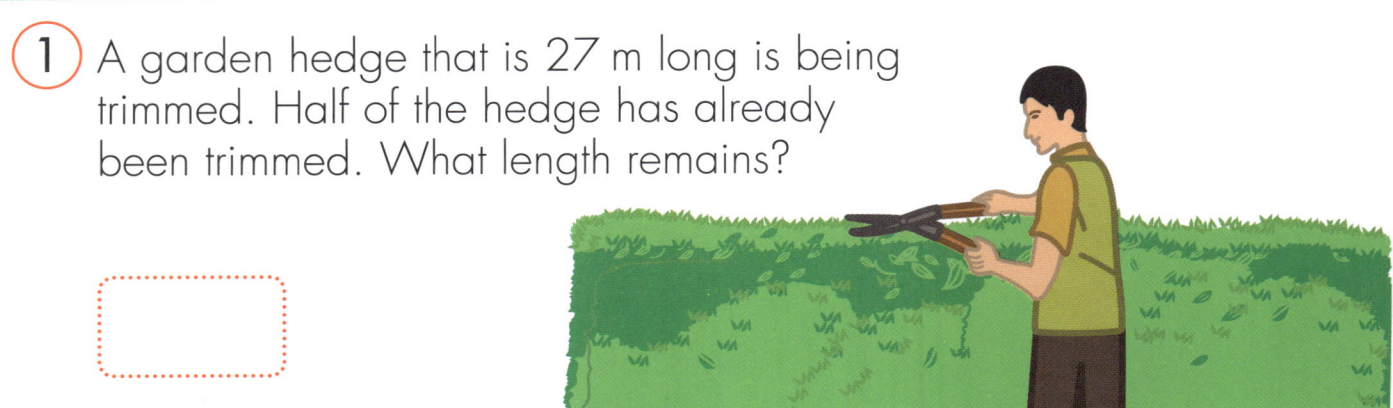

(2) Sean travelled from Winchester to Birmingham in three stages. He first travelled from Winchester to Oxford, which is a distance of 88 km away. From Oxford, he travelled 132 km to Walsall. Finally, he travelled a distance of 15 km from Walsall to Birmingham City Centre. How far has Sean travelled in total?

(3) Barbara worked out that 42 m multiplied by six is 251 m. But her answer is incorrect.

What should the answer be?

By how much was Barbara wrong?

(4) How many millimetres are equal to one metre?

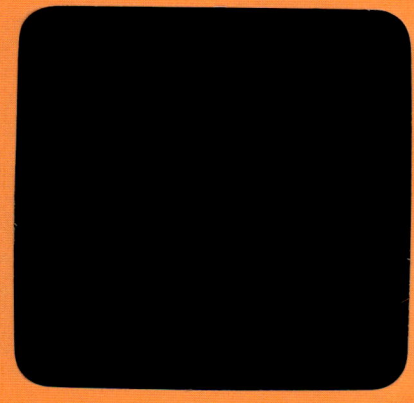

Time filler:
Use the internet to find and work out the distances in miles between some of your favourite places. Then roughly convert the miles into kilometres and check to see if you are correct.

5) Two lengths added together make a total of 1.5 m. If one length is 85 cm, what is the other? Write your answer in centimetres.

6) Darius took 10 minutes to walk 800 m. If he covered the entire distance at the same speed, how far did Darius walk in one minute?

7) A 1p coin has a diameter of 20 mm. If eight of these coins are laid in a straight line, what will be the length of this line?

8) A cow grazes a distance of 3 km each day. How far would the cow have grazed in one week?

20

Perimeter problems

Always remember to add the measurement units, such as centimetre (cm) and kilometre (km), when writing distances.

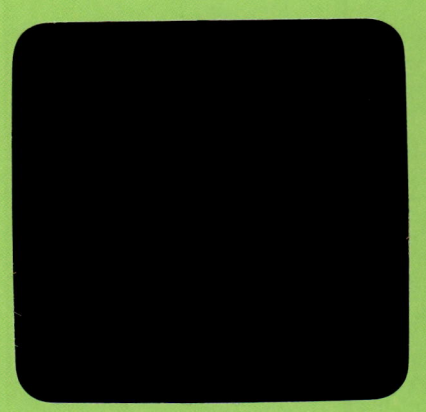

① The perimeter of a square is 64 cm. What is the length of each side?

② The perimeter of a rectangle is 36 cm. If the length of the rectangle is 12 cm, find its width.

③ The width of a rectangle is half its length. If the perimeter is 18 cm, what are the rectangle's length and width?

Length   Width

④ Emma plays netball on a court, which is 31 m long and 15 m wide. To warm up before a game, Emma ran once around the perimeter of the court. How far did Emma run?

Time filler:
Estimate the perimeter of a few rectangular objects, such as TV or computer screens and books. Write down your estimates. Then measure the objects carefully. How close were your estimates?

5 Look at the dimensions of the rectangle and find its perimeter.

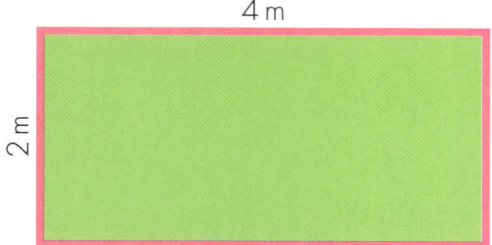

6 Look at the dimensions of the square and find its perimeter.

7 The perimeter of a square is 10 cm. Find the length of each side.

8 An ant walks around the edges of a rectangular table top. The table is 2 m long and 1 m wide. How far does the ant walk?

Areas of squares and rectangles

We always measure area using square units, such as the square centimetre (cm^2) and square metre (m^2).

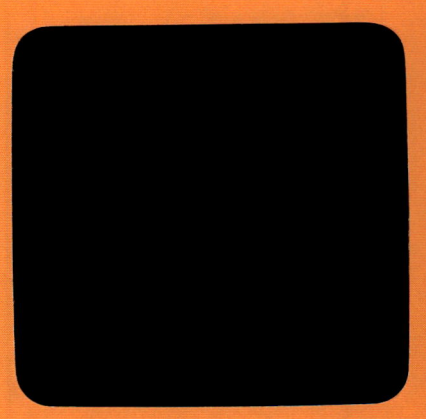

1. Karen's parents want to lay a new carpet in her bedroom. The bedroom floor is 4 m long and 3 m wide.

   What area of new carpet is required?

   If the carpet costs £10 per square metre, how much will Karen's new bedroom carpet cost?

2. A builder draws the rectangular shape of a house he plans to build on graph paper. Look at his drawing below and the scale, and then calculate the area of the proposed house.

   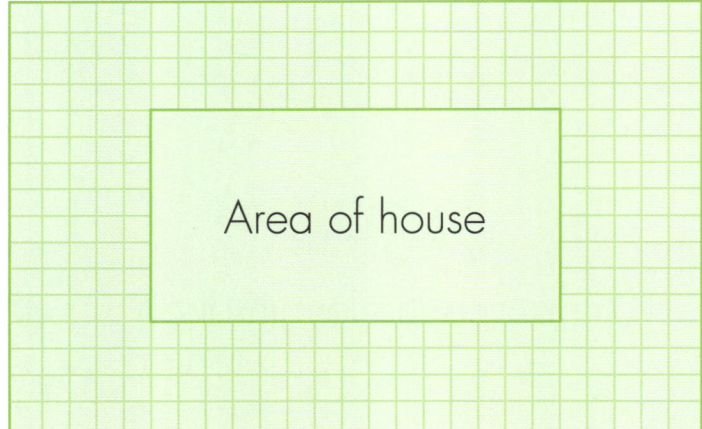

   Scale
   1 grid square = $1 m^2$

   Area of house

3. A parking space in a car park is 4 m long and 2 m wide. What is the area of the parking space?

4. A square has an area of $144 cm^2$. What is the length of each side?

Time filler:
Estimate the area of some small flat objects such as book covers in your bedroom. Write down the area of each. Now use a ruler to measure each object to work out their areas. How close were your estimates?

(5) The area of a rectangle is 72 m². If the width of the rectangle is 4 m, then what is its length?

(6) The width of a TV screen is 60 cm and the height is 35 cm. What is the area of the screen?

(7) The area of a rectangle is 32 cm². The length of the rectangle is two times its width. Calculate the length and the width of the rectangle.

Length   Width

(8) A table is placed in the centre of a carpet that has an area of 9 m². If the table has an area of 2 m², what is the area of the carpet around the table?

Areas of compound shapes

24

Look carefully at the diagrams to answer the questions.

1) Peter's mum has to lay some new turf in the garden. This diagram shows the shape she has to cover.

Scale 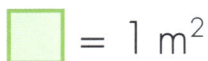 = 1 m²

Count the squares and find the area that the new turf will cover.

2) Dawn has to find the area of a shape she is using to make a model. This is the shape.

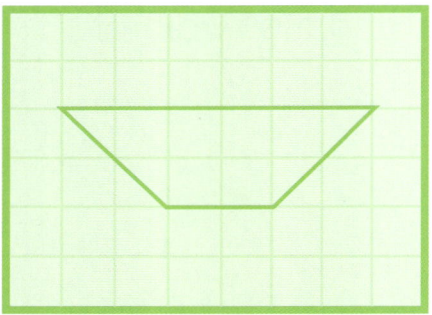

Scale  = 1 cm²

Count the squares and find the area of Dawn's shape.

3) An area of road that has been damaged by heavy rain needs to be resurfaced.

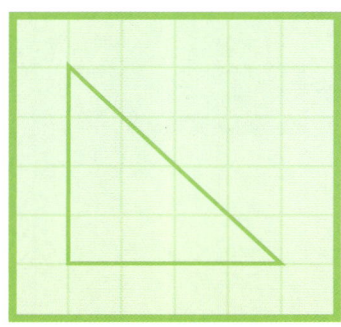

Scale  = 1 m²

The diagram shows the area that has been damaged. Count the squares to find the area of damaged road.

Time filler:
Look at any tiled areas in your house, such as in the kitchen or bathroom. See if there are any half or part squares and decide how you would count them to calculate the total area.

4 What are the areas of these shapes?

Scale
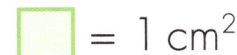 = 1 cm²

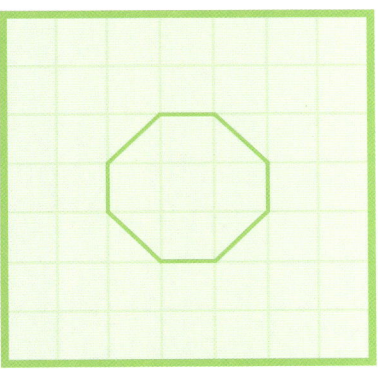

Scale
☐ = 1 cm²

5 Jack's dad has decided to renovate Jack's room. He makes the following drawing for it.

What will be the area of Jack's new room?

Scale
 = 1 m²

Weights and measures 1

Can you remember how many grams (g) there are in a kilogram (kg)?

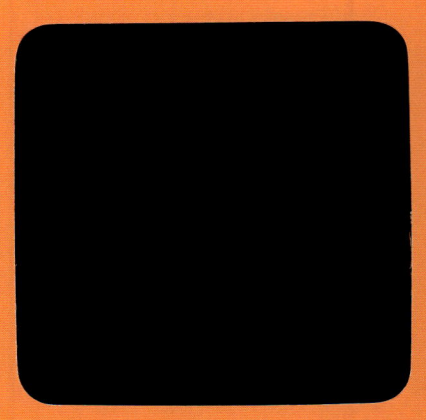

---

1 Bob uses a jug to fill up a bath with hot water. The jug can hold 3 l and Bob wants to fill the bath with 60 l of water. How many times will Bob have to fill the jug?

[ ] times

---

2 Jake has forgotten how many grams there are in a kilogram. He thinks 7 kg is the same as 700 g, which is incorrect. Can you write down the correct answer for him?

[ ]

---

3 Roz weighs 39.6 kg. Six months earlier, she weighed 33.4 kg. How much weight has Roz gained?

[ ]

---

4 Boris bought 3 kg of cherries and did a quick count to discover that there were about 60 cherries in 500 g. How many cherries does Boris have altogether?

[ ] cherries

Time filler:
Look in some recipe books to see if there is a table of units and conversions between units. You should find some unusual measuring units such as teaspoon (tsp) and tablespoon (tbsp). See how many other units you can find.

5 An ounce (oz) is about the same as 28 g. How many grams of sugar would be about the same as 4 oz of sugar?

6 One box of cereal weighs 620 g and another weighs 480 g. What is the difference in their weights?

7 How many milligrams are the same as one gram?

8 The maximum weight of a person allowed on a fairground ride at an amusement park is 50 kg. Omar weighs 25 080 g. Calculate his weight in kilograms to find out whether he will be allowed on the ride.

Weights and measures 2

Are you ready to tackle more problems about weights and measures? Let's go!

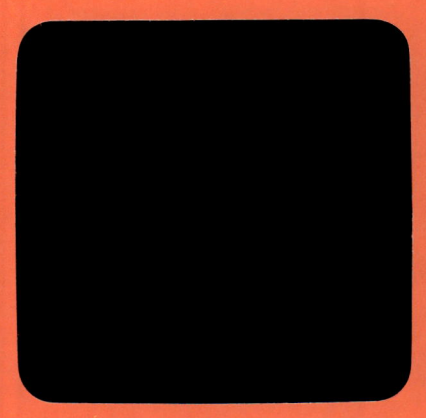

1) A cup can hold 380 ml of water. Sam is using the cup to fill a bottle for a school trip. He has filled the cup five times and poured the water into the bottle. How much water has Sam put in the bottle? Write your answer in litres.

2) An athlete is practising for a long jump competition. Her first jump is 2.65 m long and the second jump is 2.82 m long. By how much has she improved her jump?

3) What is the difference in length between 62 cm and 1.04 m? Write your answer in centimetres.

4) An Indian elephant weighs 2 800 kg. It picks up a log weighing 450 kg. What is the total weight of the elephant and the log?

Time filler:
Pour some water into a glass. Estimate the volume in millilitres and then measure the volume as accurately as you can. How close was your estimate? Find a large potato, apple or orange and estimate its weight and then weigh it. Again, how close was your estimate?

5 When Katie and her mother take their hand luggage to the airport, they are told the bag is too heavy. The bag weighs 9.3 kg but the allowance for luggage is only 6 kg. By how much have they exceeded the luggage allowance?

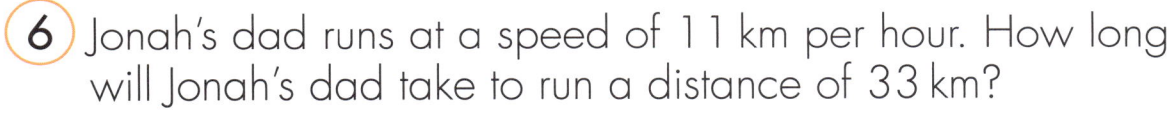

6 Jonah's dad runs at a speed of 11 km per hour. How long will Jonah's dad take to run a distance of 33 km?

7 Wendy has a 1 l shampoo bottle. She has used half of it. What's the quantity of shampoo left in the bottle? Write your answer in millilitres.

8 A teacher carried 12 books to his classroom. Each book weighed 0.1 kg. What was the total weight of the books? Write your answer in kilograms.

Money problems 2

Get ready to practise some more money problems.

1. Mirka visited a stationery shop. She bought a fancy pencil for £1.50, two marker pens for 80p each and a glue stick for £2.80. How much did Mirka pay in total?

2. Peter receives £5 pocket money each week. Last week, he bought an ice cream for £1.40, lent £2 to his sister and donated 50p to charity. He saved the rest of the money. How much did Peter manage to save?

3. Isobel's class is raising money for charity. Twenty children donated £1 each and nine children donated £1.50 each. How much money has the class raised so far?

4. Rob earns £6.50 an hour. At the end of a day, he earned £39. How many hours did Rob work that day?

Time filler:
Find out about other major currencies such as the euro (€), US dollar ($) and the Japanese Yen (¥). Invent a few sums of your own for each currency.

5) A shopping bill amounts to £56.28. A quarter of the bill has been spent on fruit. How much money has not been spent on fruit?

6) Kevin bought 2 kg tomatoes, which cost £2.20 per kg. He paid the shopkeeper £10. How much change did the shopkeeper give him?

7) If a pound is worth the same as 1.7 US dollars, what is the value of £5 in US dollars? **Note:** the sign for a dollar is $.

8) A taxi driver charges £2.30 per km. If you travel a distance of 8 km in his taxi, how much will your journey cost?

Decimals 1

Always be very careful to place the decimal point in the correct position.

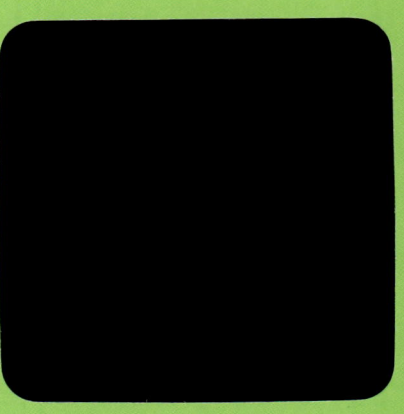

① A piece of elastic is 0.32 m long. When stretched, the elastic becomes 1.35 m long. By what length has the elastic increased from its original size?

② A cook had 1 l of milk in a carton. He used 0.65 l of it while baking a pudding. How much milk is left in the carton?

③ Add these lengths and write the answer.

3.12 m + 0.84 m + 0.09 m

④ Three boxes are stacked one on top of the other. The first box is 0.16 m high, the second 0.41 m high and the third 0.33 m high. The boxes together need to be 1 m high, but they are not. How much short of 1 m is the stack of boxes?

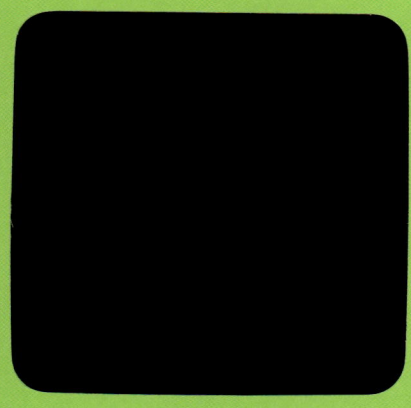

Time filler:
Measure the length of your fingernails as carefully as you can, which is probably to the nearest millimetre. Measure them again one week later to see which nails have grown the most.

⑤ How many millilitres are there in 1.425 l?

⑥ Jack, Gina and Grace did some odd jobs for their aunt to earn extra pocket money during their summer holidays. Jack cleaned the garden and earned £2, Gina washed the car and earned £2.10 and Grace painted the fence and earned £1.95. They need £6 for a new set of books they plan to buy together. How much extra money have they made?

⑦ Gill buys two large loaves of bread at £2.75 each and one pack of bagels at £1.35. How much change will she get if she pays with a £10 note?

⑧ A toy brick is 1.8 cm high. If another brick that is 3.4 cm high is placed on top of it, what will be the total height of the two bricks?

Decimals 2

Test your maths skills by adding and subtracting decimal quantities in these problems.

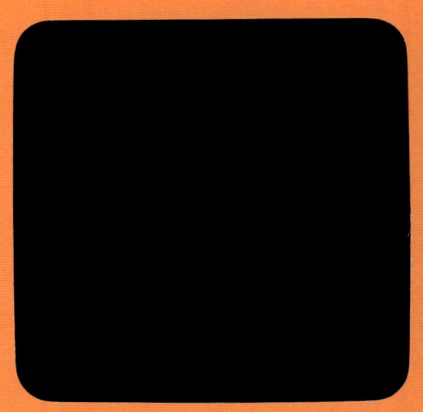

1) An athlete took part in a local triathlon. She began by running 5.4 km and then swimming 2.7 km. Finally, she cycled to the finishing line. If the total distance of the race was 10 km, how long was the cycle ride?

2) When two bags of sand are weighed together, they make up 3.65 kg. If one of the bags weighs 1.77 kg, what is the weight of the other bag?

3) A cinema ticket costs £10.50 for an adult and £7.20 for a child. If two parents take two children to see a film, what will be the total cost of the tickets?

4) A king cobra is 4.5 m long. If its head and neck region is 0.7 m long, what is the length of the rest of its body?

Time filler:
Draw five lines of different lengths on a piece of paper. Estimate the length of each line and write it down. Now measure each line accurately to see how close your estimates were.

5) An empty jar weighs 0.60 kg. When filled with sweets, it weighs 1.95 kg. How much do the sweets weigh?

6) A bus journey is a distance of 32.4 km. If 16.3 km of the journey has already been covered, how much distance is left?

7) Tim has 1.5 m of train track. Pam has 2.2 m and Sean has 0.5 m. If they join their tracks together, how long will their combined track be?

8) Four children had a total of £6.50. Together, they spent £3.60 on ice cream. What is the amount of money left?

Fractions

A very good knowledge of times tables will help you with these problems.

(1) A class has 30 children. Half of the children have brown eyes and one-third have green eyes. How many children do not have brown or green eyes?

 children

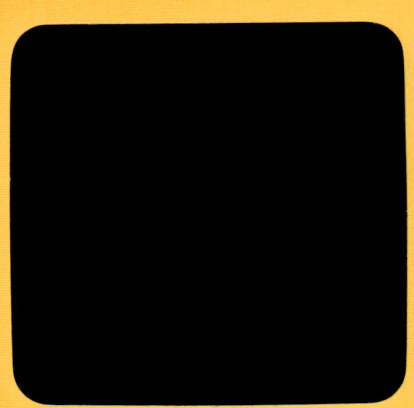

(2) In a packet of sweets, one-fifth are peanut butter flavoured and one-tenth are blueberry flavoured. The packet has 40 sweets.

How many of them are peanut butter sweets? sweets

How many of them are blueberry sweets? sweets

How many sweets have neither the peanut butter nor the blueberry flavour? sweets

(3) Harris has 36 comics. If he gives one-sixth of these to Anne, how many comics will he be left with? comics

(4) Vikki has travelled 12 km of her journey. If she has covered one-tenth of the journey, what is the total distance?

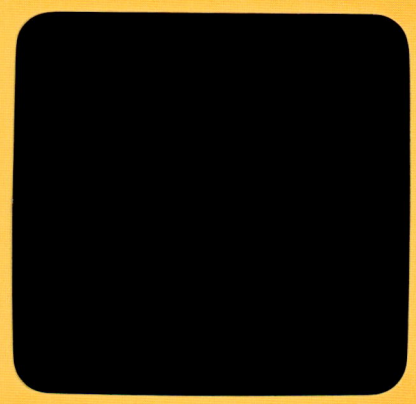

Time filler:
Use a TV guide and look at any four-hour period of programmes. Work out roughly what fraction belongs to each of these categories: news, sports, drama and comedy. Now check again for a different four-hour period and see if they match.

5) Daisy collects plastic animals and has 56 of them. She works out that one-seventh of the animals are birds. How many of them are not birds?    animals

6) Nancy's dad gave her £18. He asked her to donate one-third of it to charity. How much money will Nancy be left with after making the donation?

7) Peter is growing tired of his road trip and asks his father how far they have travelled. Peter's father says the journey is 80 km and they have travelled one-eighth of it. How far does Peter still have to go?

8) Serena's brother has a Saturday-morning job as a paperboy. He has to deliver 250 newspapers. Fifty of them are delivered in the same street. What fraction of the newspapers is that?

Fractions and percentages

It is important to know simple fractions and their percentage equivalents.

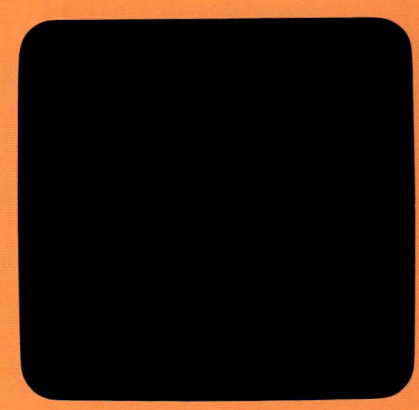

1) Clara attempted 20 questions in a test. Seventy-five percent of her answers were correct. How many of Clara's answers were incorrect?

 answers

2) A loaf of bread has 28 slices. Twenty-five percent of the slices are used to make sandwiches and $\frac{1}{3}$ of the rest are used to make toast. How many slices have not been used?

 slices

3) On Jane's birthday, 85% of her cake was eaten. What percentage of the cake was left?

4) One-tenth of Kyle's books are picture books, two-tenths are storybooks and half are science fiction. The remaining books are encyclopedias. What fraction of Kyle's books are encyclopedias?

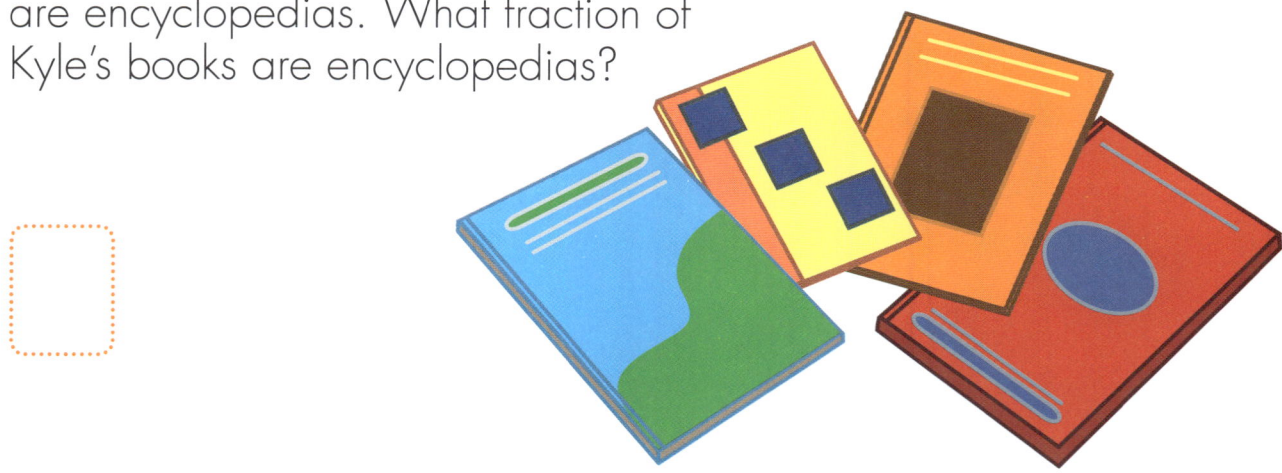

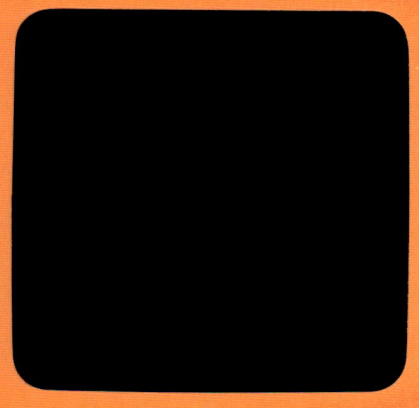

Time filler:
Look at some of the cartons and packets of food, such as milk and cereal, in your kitchen. Find the weight or volume of each one (printed on the label). Then work out the measurements for 25%, 50% and 75% of the contents.

(5) Out of 40 bananas, two-fifths are not ripe enough to be eaten. How many bananas can be eaten?

☐ bananas

(6) Sam gets £5 pocket money. She spends 40% of it on a book. How much money does she spend?

(7) There are 240 passengers travelling on a plane. Four-eighths of them are women, three-eighths are men and one-eighth are children. How many of each of these three groups are there on the plane?

☐ women

☐ men

☐ children

(8) Tim exercises for two hours every day. He spends 25% of the time jogging. How much time does he spend jogging each day? Answer in minutes.

(9) One morning, 20% of the students in a class were absent. What fraction of students is that?

40

Understanding graphs 1

Always look very carefully at the information shown on a graph to solve the problems based on it.

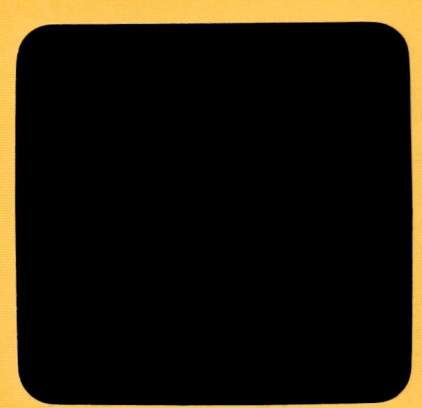

Look at the graph below and answer the questions that follow.

Time taken travelling to school

Time in minutes (y-axis: 5, 10, 15, 20, 25)

- Bob: 5
- Sandra: 25
- Ted: 20
- Alice: 5
- Mary: 15

Children

(1) What is the total time taken by all the children travelling to school?

(2) Which children take more time than Mary?

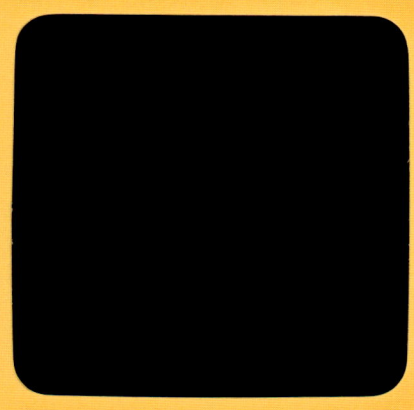

Time filler:
Sketch a graph to show some information about the children in your class. For example, the graph could show height or number of brothers and sisters. Make sure the graph is labelled clearly.

3) Which two children take the same amount of time travelling to school?

4) Which child takes the most time to reach school?

How long does he or she travel for?

5) How much longer than Ted does Sandra take?

6) If Ted cycles to school, he will take half the time to get there. How long will it take Ted to cycle to school?

7) How much longer than Alice does Mary take?

8) One day, Sandra gets a lift and it takes her only five minutes to reach school. How much time has Sandra managed to save that day?

Understanding graphs 2

Always make sure your bar charts are clearly labelled.

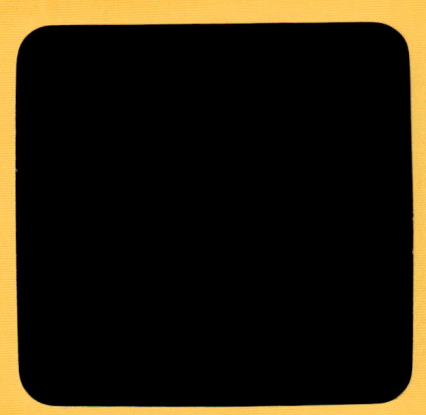

Ross wanted to find out what his friends ate for breakfast. He asked eight friends and noted down what they had eaten that morning. The data below shows the information he collected.

Number of friends	Type of breakfast
4	Cereal
1	Boiled egg
1	Fruit
2	Toast

1 Draw and label a bar chart to show Ross's information.

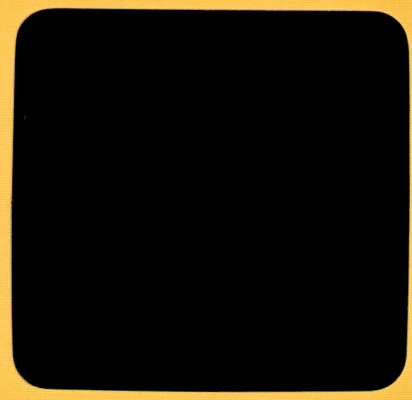

Time filler:
Information, or data, is not always shown in bar charts. Look in magazines, books or on the internet to see how many other kinds of charts you can find.

2 What fraction of Ross's friends ate cereal for breakfast?

3 What fraction did not have toast?

4 How many friends did not have cereal?

☐ friends

5 How many friends ate a boiled egg or fruit?

☐ friends

What fraction is that?

6 What fraction ate cereal, a boiled egg or toast?

Addition and subtraction 1

When you have finished each sum, double-check the answer.

1) Rashid, Sabah and Michael are saving 1p coins for charity. In six months, Rashid has collected 92 coins, Sabah 85 coins and Michael 103 coins. How much money have they collected in total? Write your answer in pounds.

2) Farmer Frank has put his cattle into barns for winter. He moved 52 cows from one field, 45 cows from another field and 37 cows from a third field. Each barn can hold 40 cows. How many barns did Frank use?

_____ barns

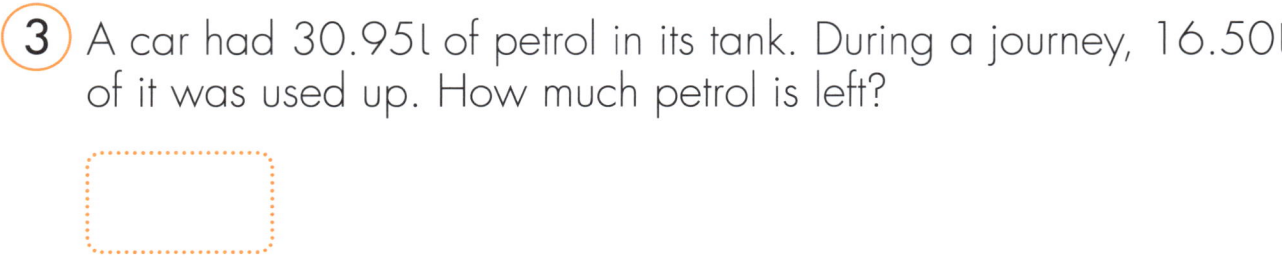

3) A car had 30.95l of petrol in its tank. During a journey, 16.50l of it was used up. How much petrol is left?

4) Three consecutive numbers (numbers in a row) add up to 21. What are the numbers?

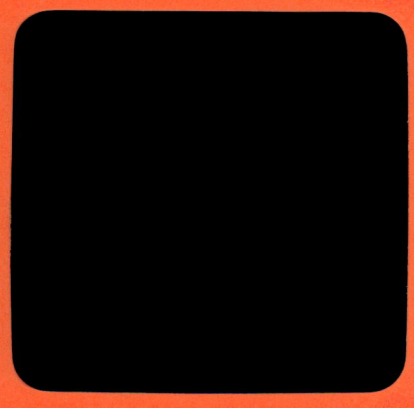

Time filler:
A good way to check answers is to do the reverse operation. For example, if six plus seven is 13 then 13 minus six should be seven. Write five sums of your own, work them out and check each of them by doing the reverse operation.

5 Two suitcases are put on weighing scales at an airport check-in counter. One suitcase weighs 12.8 kg and the total weight of both of them is 23 kg. How much does the other suitcase weigh?

6 One thousand pamphlets were printed for a local museum. Of these, 725 are colour and the rest are black and white. How many black-and-white pamphlets were printed?

pamphlets

7 Jan thinks of a number. She adds 25 to it and then subtracts six. Her final number is 69. What number did Jan start with?

8 When Becky first played a computer game, she scored 478 points. On her second attempt, she scored 680 points. How many more points did Becky score on her second attempt?

points

Addition and subtraction 2

Don't expect all sums to be straightforward. You might have to be a very clever thinker!

1 When David added three numbers together, he arrived at a total of 68. One of the numbers is 12 and the second number is its double. What is David's third number?

2 Emmie has a collection of 600 CDs. She has decided to give some away to charity. If Emmie gives away 48 CDs, how many will she have left?

_____ CDs

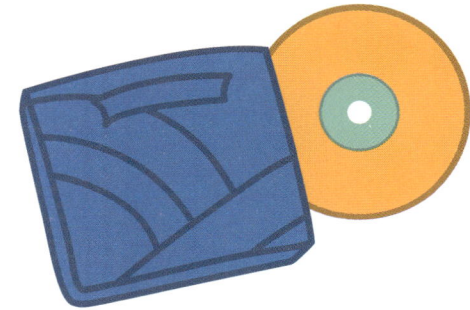

3 Sean wants to give some money to the school fund. He finds 78 p in his wallet and 54 p in his bedroom drawer. He then decides to give £1 of the money to the fund. How much money will Sean keep for himself?

4 The total of three numbers is 1 000. If 80 and 250 are two of the numbers, what is the third number?

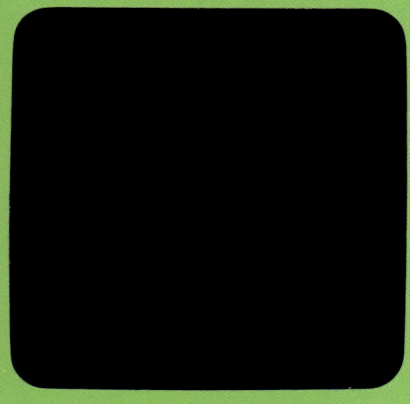

Time filler:
Write down any random numbers in numerical order, add them up and write the answer. Now add them up again, but this time in the reverse order. Is the answer the same? You might have made a mistake. This is another good way to check your answers.

5) In a tin of 90 biscuits, 34 have been broken. How many biscuits are not broken?

☐ biscuits

6) Petra's mum has 86 emails in her inbox, but 49 of them are unwanted spam. How many emails are not spam?

☐ emails

7) Gaia added two numbers together and the sum came to 240. If one of the numbers is 165, what is the other number?

☐

8) Seventy pages of a notebook have been used up. If the notebook has 130 pages, how many blank pages are left?

☐ pages

Multiplication and division 1

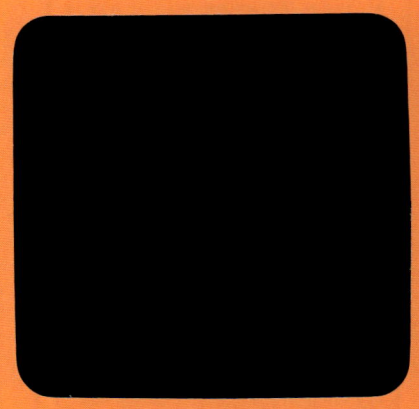

Have a go at these problems to brush up your multiplication and division skills.

1) In a video game, a player is awarded 15 points every time the frog catches a fly and 20 points when the frog catches a wasp. How many points will a player earn if the frog catches six flies and nine wasps?

[ ] points

2) Charlie has been saving money to buy his sister a present. He has saved 50 p every day for 21 days. How much money has he saved?

[ ]

3) A teacher marked 64 test booklets every evening for six days. How many booklets did the teacher mark in total?

[ ] booklets

4) Pat went to the gym 132 times in a year. How many times did she go each month?

[ ] times

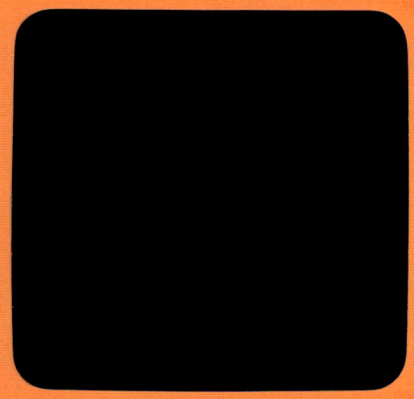

Time filler:
Sharpen your mental arithmetic. Think of any number between 12 and 20 and write it down. Now work out several multiples of this number in your head. Do the same with a couple of other numbers.

5 A parcel delivery company has 520 parcels to be delivered by four drivers. How many parcels will each driver need to deliver?

☐ parcels

6 Victor thinks of a number that is seven times smaller than 56. Which number did he think of?

☐

7 Debbie multiplied a number by itself and got 81 as the product. Which number did Debbie start with?

☐

8 A birthday cake is covered with chocolate buttons and cut into eight pieces. Each piece has 6 buttons except one piece, which has 7. How many chocolate buttons were put on the cake?

☐ buttons

Multiplication and division 2

A very good knowledge of times tables will help you with these problems.

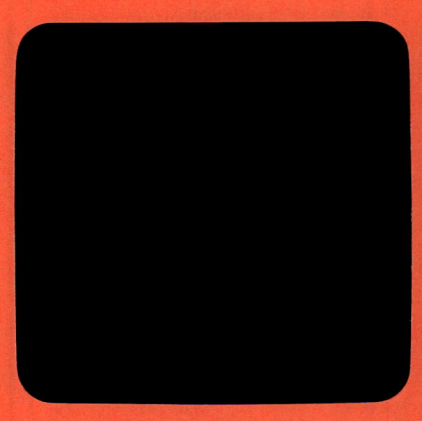

1. A teacher started a maths lesson by writing 10 sums on the board and asking the students to solve them. In the evening, the teacher checked the answers. If the class has 30 children, how many answers did the teacher have to mark?

   ☐ answers

2. Mrs Harris has collected 68 fridge magnets over the years. She decides to buy a smaller fridge, so she distributes the magnets equally between Molly, Isaac, Louis and Isobel. How many fridge magnets does each child receive?

   ☐ magnets

3. A driver collects 10 vouchers every time he spends £1 on petrol. In one week, the driver spent £55 on petrol. If each voucher is worth 2p, how much did the driver earn in vouchers that week?

   ☐

4. Felt-tip pens come in packets of 20. How many pens will there be in a dozen packets?

   ☐ pens

Time filler:
Write down the values of all the coins between 1p and £1. Now multiply each value by 12 and write down the answer. Finally, divide each amount by four and write the answer.

5) Kim divided a number by 12 and arrived at an answer of 15. What number did Kim start with?

6) The captain of a ship loaded 600 containers in 12 rows. How many containers are there in each row?

containers

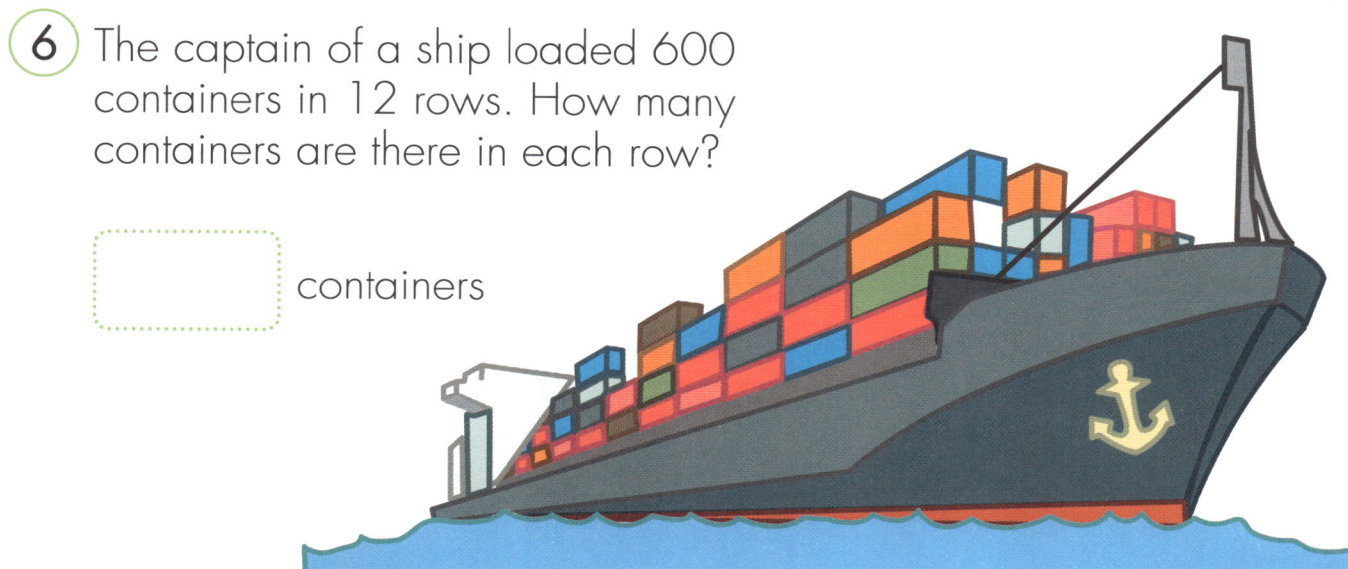

7) Ninety sweets are divided among a number of children. If each child receives 15 sweets, how many children are there?

children

8) Eighty-four bananas are shared equally among 12 people. How many bananas does each person get?

bananas

Money problems 3

By now, you will find these money problems pretty easy to work out.

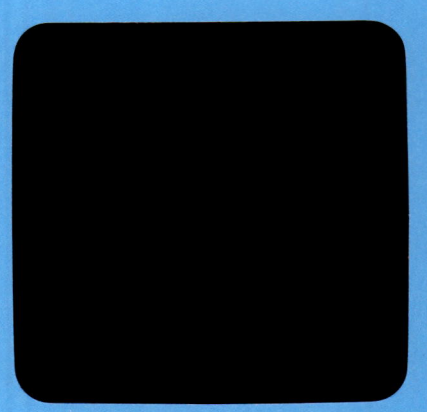

1) Convert these amounts of money from pence to pounds.

1 000 p   ......

700 p   ......

250 p   ......

100 p   ......

2) £4 was shared equally among 5 children. How much money did each child receive?   ......

3) William and Kate added their money together and then shared it equally among themselves and their son George. If William had £3.50 and Kate had £5.50, how much money did George receive after the money was shared equally among the three of them?

......

4) Claire, Bruno, Mark and Ella went for lunch together. They shared the bill of £20.60 equally among themselves. How much money did each of them pay?

......

Time filler:
Use the internet to find the conversion rate between the British pound (£) and the euro (€). Now convert some money from pounds to euros to see how much you would have if you lived somewhere in the Eurozone, such as France or Ireland.

5) How many £5 notes make up £100?

☐ notes

6) Sarah travels to school by bus. A return ticket costs her £1.30 per day. If Sarah goes to school five days a week, how much does she spend on bus tickets each week?

☐

7) Dan collected £3.60 for charity. His mum said she would give him twice the amount of money he collected.

How much money will his mum give him? ☐

How much money would Dan have collected in total? ☐

8) David got £200 as a birthday present. He bought himself two new computer games that cost £49.99 each.

How much did the two games cost in total? ☐

How much money does David have left after buying the two games? ☐

Times tables problems 1

54

You must be able to recall all your times tables instantly to do these questions.

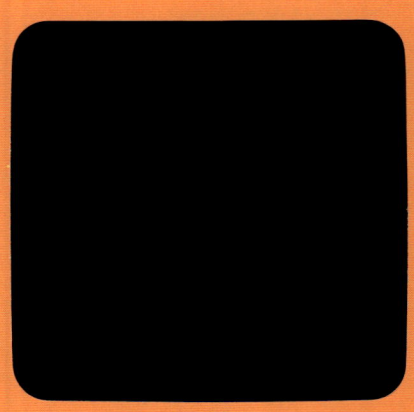

(1) Billy is 7 years old and Mandy is 12 years old. How many months old are they?

Billy is ☐ months old   Mandy is ☐ months old

(2) A paperboy earns £7 per day.

If he works five days a week, how much will he earn? ☐

He can earn £12 per day if he works on Saturday and Sunday. How much would he earn in a week if he worked at the weekend, too? ☐

(3) It costs Emmie £12 each time she has a piano lesson. If Emmie has nine lessons, how much will they cost her?

☐

In the Summer term, the cost of each lesson drops. If Emmie has eight lessons then and they cost her £72, how much does each lesson cost?

☐

Time filler:
Write down these numbers: 24, 60, 72, 90. Write down their multiplication combinations. For example, 72 can be an answer to 6 x 12 as well as 2 x 36.

④ For a party, five children collect eight pairs of sunglasses each. How many pairs of sunglasses do they have altogether?

[   ] pairs of sunglasses

⑤ How many days are there in nine weeks?

[   ] days

⑥ Seven children have collected eight party hats each. What is the total number of hats they have for the party?

[   ] hats

⑦ How many months are there in five years?

[   ] months

⑧ A teacher has drawn six octagons on the board. How many sides has he drawn in total?

[   ] sides

Times tables problems 2

Remember, times tables help with multiplication, division and fractions!

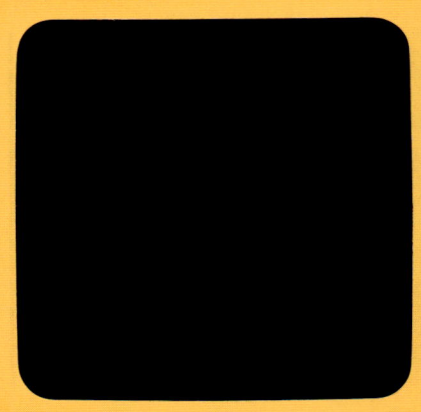

① Daniel bought eight boxes of chocolates to take on a holiday. Each box contains 12 chocolates. How many chocolates does Daniel have in total?

☐ chocolates

② William multiplied two by three. He multiplied the answer by four and then doubled it. Finally, he divided that answer by four. Which number did William finish with?

☐

③ Adam believes only two single-digit numbers can be multiplied to make 63, but he cannot remember the numbers. Help Adam find out what the two numbers are.

☐ and ☐

④ Sarah doubled a number. She then doubled the result and got 32. Which number did Sarah start with?

☐

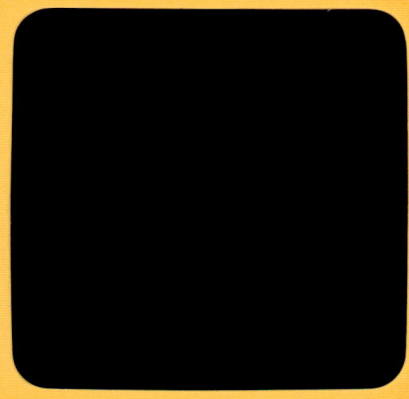

Time filler:
Some numbers can only be a multiple of either one or themselves. For example, 1 x 7 = 7. Find five other such numbers. These numbers are called prime numbers.

5) Which number multiplied by four gives the same answer as six times six?

6) The product of which two single-digit numbers gives 35?

[ ] and [ ]

7) Multiply the number of days in a week by the number of months in a year.

8) A packet contains eight biscuits. Lorraine wants 48 biscuits to share with her friends. How many packets will she need?

Ratio problems 1

Ratios are a way of showing the relationships between amounts. Have a go at these problems.

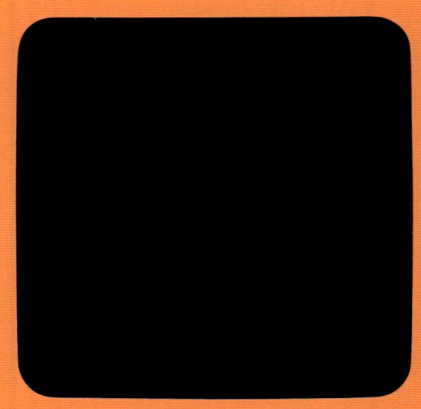

① An artist made pink paint by adding one part of red paint to three parts of white paint. If the artist uses 36 parts of white paint, how much red paint will he need?

☐ parts

② In a class of 24 children, one in every three children is a girl.

What fraction of the class is boys? ☐

How many girls are there? ☐

③ A car dealer has 50 cars. Out of every 10 cars, two are white and three are red. How many cars of those colours are there?

☐ red cars   ☐ white cars

④ For every oak tree in a forest, there are three ash trees. If the forest has 24 oak trees, find the number of ash trees.

☐ ash trees

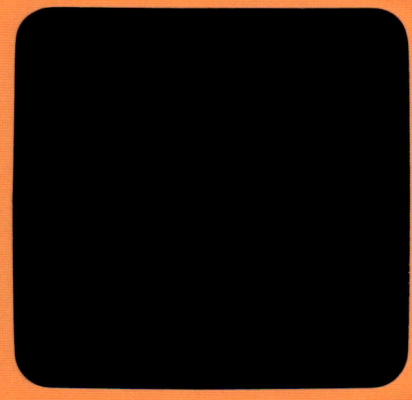

Time filler:
Find out the following ratios at home. The ratio of male to female members of your family, the ratio of people to mugs and the ratio of TVs to people.

5) A decorator uses eight cans of white paint to every three cans of magnolia paint. If the decorator uses 24 cans of magnolia paint, how many cans of white paint will he use?

☐ cans

6) For every magpie seen in a garden, there are six swallows. If 42 swallows have been seen, how many magpies will have been seen?

☐ magpies

7) Mum gives Clara three times as many cherries as she gives Oliver. If Oliver has eight cherries, how many does Clara have?

☐ cherries

8) John is twice as old as Laura and Laura is twice as old as Sally. If Sally is seven years old, how old is John?

☐ years

Ratio problems 2

Try and imagine each situation to help you understand exactly what is happening and what you need to find out.

① Children at a school were asked if they could play a musical instrument. For every three children that could play the guitar, there was one that could play the piano. If there are thirteen pianists at the school, how many guitarists are there?

☐ guitarists

② For every five boxes of cereal bought, a supermarket hands out a free tub of ice cream. If a man buys 15 boxes of cereal, how many free tubs of ice cream will he receive?

☐ tubs

③ A painter mixed paints in the proportion of five parts white to two parts blue to one part yellow. If he used 20 parts white paint, how many parts blue and yellow did the painter use?

☐ parts blue   ☐ parts yellow

④ Bricklayers mix four bags of sand to one bag of cement. If they use eight bags of cement, how many bags of sand will they need?

☐ bags of sand

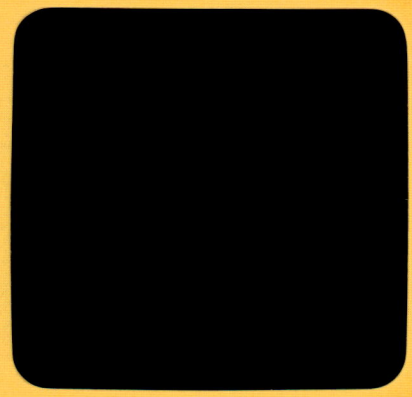

Time filler:
Think about the children in your class. Work out five ratios about your classmates, such as brown hair:blond hair or blue eyes:brown eyes.

5) The teacher tells the students that three in every eight cats are male. If the students study 24 cats, how many of them should be male and how many female?

☐ male cats   ☐ female cats

6) For every yellow clay brick that Maggie has, she has seven blue ones. If Maggie has 56 blue bricks, how many yellow bricks does she have?

☐ yellow bricks

7) The ratio of the weight of Ryan's cat to the weight of Kim's cat is three to four. If Ryan's cat weighs 6 kg, how much does Kim's cat weigh?

☐

8) In a class of 30 children, two out of every three children have brown hair. The rest have blond hair. How many children have brown hair and how many of them have blond hair?

☐ have brown hair   ☐ have blond hair

Harder problems 1

Are you ready for these brainteasers? You've had lots of practice, so let's go!

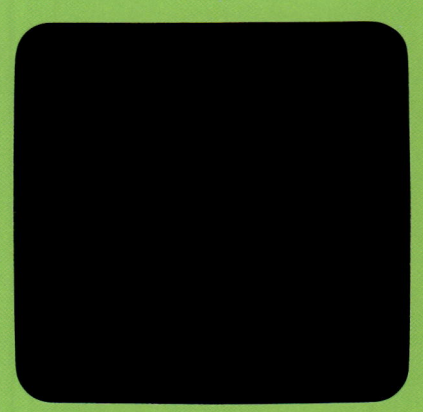

1. A number is multiplied by its double and the answer is 72. What is the number?

2. A farmer has 180 ewes on his farm. In spring, each of them gives birth to two lambs. How many ewes and lambs will there now be on the farm?

☐ ewes and lambs

3. The sum of two numbers is 15. The product of these numbers is 54. What are the two numbers?

☐ and ☐

4. Martin and Marie go jogging together. Martin runs twice as far as Marie. If they cover a total distance of 12 km together, how far does each of them run?

Martin ☐

Marie ☐

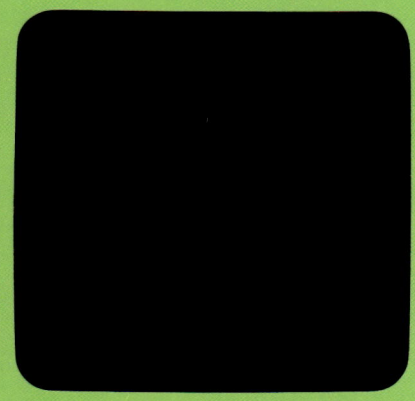

Time filler:
Write some number problems of your own and ask your family members to solve them. You can make them as tricky as you like! You could give a prize to the fastest solver!

⑤ James spends 68p on sweets. He pays for it with a £1 coin and receives three different coins as change. What are the values of the coins?

☐ ☐ ☐

⑥ A number is doubled first and then doubled again. All three numbers are then added together and the total is 49. What is the original number?

⑦ Cathy and Sean go fishing and catch 12 fish altogether. If Cathy catches three times as many fish as Sean, how many fish does each child catch?

Cathy catches ☐ fish

Sean catches ☐ fish

⑧ The total of two numbers is 21 and the difference between them is three. What are the two numbers?

☐ and ☐

Harder problems 2

Read the wording very carefully and decide what needs to be done.

1. Find the total of these numbers. Can you work out a quick way of adding them?

   0, 1, 2, 3, 4, 5, 6, 7, 8, 9, 10

2. Allie multiplied a number by itself and then halved it. The answer was 60.5. Which number did Allie begin with?

3. On a typical day, Dr Foster spends eight minutes with each patient and then has a break for two minutes. How many patients can Dr Foster see each hour?

   _____ patients

4. Corey went to watch the latest animated film, which is 1 hour 55 minutes long. The film ended at 1.30 p.m. What time did it begin?

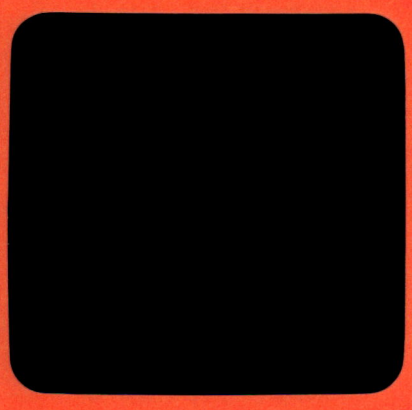

Time filler:
Look at this sum: 12 + 3 − 4 + 5 + 67 + 8 + 9 = 100. What do you notice? Look on the internet for more fun maths facts. Can you find out the name for the massive number that is one followed by one hundred zeroes?

5) Peter spends twice as much on chocolates as Marilyn does. If Marilyn spends £1.65, how much do they spend in total?

6) The distance between two cities is 152 km. If your dad makes the journey in four equal stages, what distance is each stage?

7) Marianne goes to bed at 21:30 and sleeps for 10 hours. What time does Marianne wake up? Write your answer using the 24-hour format.

8) Zen makes some juice by mixing three parts orange juice with two parts water. If Zen uses 450 ml of water, how much orange juice will he need?

Answers:

04–05 Seconds, minutes and hours
06–07 Days, weeks and months

4

1. How many seconds are there in one hour?
   3 600 seconds

2. How many minutes are there in one day?
   1 440 minutes

3. Amir takes 20 minutes to walk to school and his sister Cala takes 25 minutes to walk the same distance. When their father takes them to school by car, the journey takes only six minutes. How much faster is the car journey for each child?
   Amir gains **14 minutes**   Cala gains **19 minutes**

4. Sam takes 1 hour 50 minutes to walk home. It is five times quicker for him if he takes a bus home. How long will Sam take to reach home by bus?
   22 minutes

5

5. Add together the number of minutes in one hour, three-quarters of an hour, half an hour and a quarter of an hour.
   150 minutes

6. Terry likes his eggs to be boiled for 270 seconds. How long is that in minutes and seconds?
   4 minutes 30 seconds

7. Henri and Françoise play a computer game and use a timer to record their time taken. Henri completes the game in 2 minutes 38 seconds and Françoise completes it in 1 minute 42 seconds. How much quicker is Françoise than Henri?
   56 seconds

8. It takes Dani 3 hours 45 minutes to complete the first ten levels of a new game. Alexander, however, completes them in only 55 minutes. How much quicker was Alexander than Dani?
   2 hours 50 minutes

Your child should learn simple multiples of 60 and 24 such as 5 x 60 and 8 x 24 to be able to quickly convert between minutes and seconds, hours and minutes and days and hours.

6

1. Daisy's grandmother gives her 50 p every week as pocket money. If Daisy has collected £4 without spending any money, for how many months has she been getting money from her grandmother?
   2 months

2. Mario takes four days to travel to a holiday resort with his parents. He stays at the resort for 11 days and returns home by a different route, which takes only two days. How long is the whole trip in weeks and days?
   2 weeks 3 days

3. Bogdan wants to travel the world and begins by spending 12 weeks in Poland. He then spends 24 weeks in the United States, eight weeks in Australia and 12 weeks in China. Lastly, he spends four weeks in South Africa before returning home. How long does Bogdan spend travelling? Write your answer in months.
   15 months

4. Add together the number of days in the months of May, June and July.
   92 days

7

5. List the months that have 30 days, the months that have 31 days and the month that usually has 28 days.
   Months with 30 days __April, June, September and November__
   Months with 31 days __January, March, May, July, August, October and December__
   The month with 28 days usually __February__

6. Bella has tests coming up in four weeks' time. She decides to revise five days each week and take the remaining days of the week off. How many days will Bella spend doing her revision?
   20 days

7. How many months are there in 12 years?
   144 months

8. A sailor has been on a ship for 60 days. How many weeks and days is that?
   8 weeks 4 days

Your child should readily know the number of days in each month of the year. He or she should also be able to quickly change a certain number of days into weeks. For example, 63 days can be converted into 9 weeks.

Answers:

08–09 Years, decades and centuries
10–11 The 24-hour clock

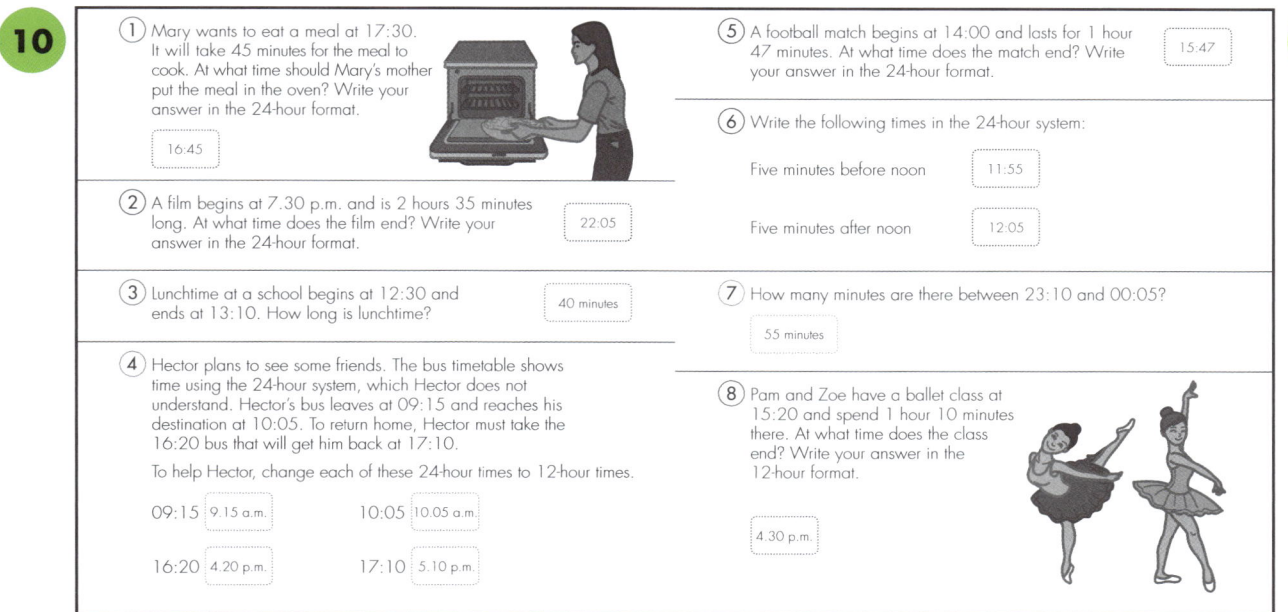

8

1) A crack in a wall widens by about 1 cm each year. If the crack is 3 cm wide now, how wide will it be after…

   1 year? **4 cm**   1 decade? **13 cm**

2) Jacob was born in 2004.

   How old will Jacob be in the year 2017? **13** years

   In which decade will Jacob be 50? **2050s**

3) Here is a list of some famous events in British history. Look at the years in which they happened. Write the year a century before and a century after each event.

Event	Year	Century before	Century after
Battle of Hastings	1066	966	1166
Great Fire of London	1666	1566	1766
Beginning of World War I	1914	1814	2014

9

4) What is the year a decade before each of these years?

   2008 **1998**   1990 **1980**   2003 **1993**

5) What is the year a decade after each of these years?

   1972 **1982**   1995 **2005**   2015 **2025**

6) What is the year a century before each of these years?

   1918 **1818**   1999 **1899**   2015 **1915**

7) What is the year a century after each of these years?

   980 **1080**   1999 **2099**   1968 **2068**

8) What name do we give to a period of 1000 years? **a millennium**

Your child should have the idea of years, decades and centuries at his or her fingertips. It is also useful if he or she knows how to write numbers and years in Roman numerals.

10

1) Mary wants to eat a meal at 17:30. It will take 45 minutes for the meal to cook. At what time should Mary's mother put the meal in the oven? Write your answer in the 24-hour format. **16:45**

2) A film begins at 7.30 p.m. and is 2 hours 35 minutes long. At what time does the film end? Write your answer in the 24-hour format. **22:05**

3) Lunchtime at a school begins at 12:30 and ends at 13:10. How long is lunchtime? **40 minutes**

4) Hector plans to see some friends. The bus timetable shows time using the 24-hour system, which Hector does not understand. Hector's bus leaves at 09:15 and reaches his destination at 10:05. To return home, Hector must take the 16:20 bus that will get him back at 17:10.

   To help Hector, change each of these 24-hour times to 12-hour times.

   09:15 **9.15 a.m.**   10:05 **10.05 a.m.**
   16:20 **4.20 p.m.**   17:10 **5.10 p.m.**

11

5) A football match begins at 14:00 and lasts for 1 hour 47 minutes. At what time does the match end? Write your answer in the 24-hour format. **15:47**

6) Write the following times in the 24-hour system:

   Five minutes before noon **11:55**

   Five minutes after noon **12:05**

7) How many minutes are there between 23:10 and 00:05? **55 minutes**

8) Pam and Zoe have a ballet class at 15:20 and spend 1 hour 10 minutes there. At what time does the class end? Write your answer in the 12-hour format. **4.30 p.m.**

It is very useful in daily life for your child to be able to switch easily and quickly between the 12-hour and 24-hour system and convert one to the other as second nature.

Answers:

12–13 More time problems
14–15 Money problems 1, see p.80
16–17 Length problems 1

12

① Two teachers recorded the time taken by children in a race. One teacher recorded the time in minutes and seconds and the other recorded it in seconds. The table below shows the results.

Name	Time taken
Stuart	2 minutes 5 seconds
Li	120 seconds
Mona	172 seconds
Zan	1 minute 55 seconds

Look at the results and find out who won the race. **Zan**

How much longer did Stuart take than Li? **5 seconds**

② Sophie and Jake have to travel from London to Birmingham. The journey should take about 2 hours 10 minutes. If Sophie and Jake leave London at 11.35 a.m., what time will they arrive in Birmingham? **1.45 p.m.**

③ What is 50 hours in days and hours? **2 days 2 hours**

④ A snail took eight hours to travel 1 m. How long did the snail take to travel each 10 cm? **48 minutes**

13

⑤ A train left Winchester at 10:03. Before reaching London Waterloo, the train waited at a signal for eight minutes. It arrived at London Waterloo at 11:05. If the train had not stopped at the signal, how long would the journey have taken? **54 minutes**

⑥ How many hours are the same as 300 minutes? **5 hours**

⑦ Which is longer: 170 seconds or 2 minutes 40 seconds? **170 seconds**

⑧ Darius and Emma have a 10-week holiday between leaving college and going to university. Their holiday begins in the first week of July.

In which month will their holiday end? **September**

In which month will they be halfway through their holiday? **August**

It is important to try and visualise the situations represented in each maths problem. If your child can imagine the scenario, he or she is more likely to solve the problem.

16

① John has a model racetrack that is 3 m long. During the school holidays, John plans to double its length. How long will the new track be? **6 m**

② Gary's father covers 10 laps of a running track every day for one week. The track is 0.4 km long. What distance does Gary's father run in one week? **28 km**

③ Convert each of these lengths into millimetres.
2.5 m — **2 500 mm**
3.1 m — **3 100 mm**
0.075 m — **75 mm**

④ A mile is about 1.6 km. How far would 5 miles be in kilometres? **8 km**

17

⑤ How many centimetres are equal to 1 km? **100 000 cm**

⑥ Add these lengths and write the answer in millimetres.
2.5 cm + 12 mm + 3.4 cm **71 mm**

⑦ Anne's parents measure her height on her birthday every year. On her sixth birthday, Anne was 111 cm tall and by her seventh birthday she was 9 cm taller. On her eighth birthday, she had grown another 10 cm. How tall was Anne on her eighth birthday? **130 cm**

⑧ Write these distances in metres.
2.5 km — **2 500 m**
160 cm — **1.6 m**
31 km — **31 000 m**

Your child should be familiar with smaller distances but may be unsure about the length of a kilometre. Go for a walk with your child and show him or her how you use a pedometer to measure a distance of 1 km.

Answers:

18–19 Length problems 2
20–21 Perimeter problems

18

1. A garden hedge that is 27 m long is being trimmed. Half of the hedge has already been trimmed. What length remains?
   13.5 m

2. Sean travelled from Winchester to Birmingham in three stages. He first travelled from Winchester to Oxford, which is a distance of 88 km away. From Oxford, he travelled 132 km to Walsall. Finally, he travelled a distance of 15 km from Walsall to Birmingham City Centre. How far has Sean travelled in total?
   235 km

3. Barbara worked out that 42 m multiplied by six is 251 m. But her answer is incorrect.
   What should the answer be? 252 m
   By how much was Barbara wrong? 1 m

4. How many millimetres are equal to one metre? 1 000 mm

19

5. Two lengths added together make a total of 1.5 m. If one length is 85 cm, what is the other? Write your answer in centimetres.
   65 cm

6. Darius took 10 minutes to walk 800 m. If he covered the entire distance at the same speed, how far did Darius walk in one minute?
   80 m

7. A 1p coin has a diameter of 20 mm. If eight of these coins are laid in a straight line, what will be the length of this line?
   160 mm

8. A cow grazes a distance of 3 km each day. How far would the cow have grazed in one week?
   21 km

Although kilometres are normally used to teach measurements in schools, most distances on signs and maps are still shown in miles in the UK. Make sure your child knows the kilometre equivalent of a mile and can convert approximately between the two.

20

1. The perimeter of a square is 64 cm. What is the length of each side?
   16 cm

2. The perimeter of a rectangle is 36 cm. If the length of the rectangle is 12 cm, find its width.
   6 cm

3. The width of a rectangle is half its length. If the perimeter is 18 cm, what are the rectangle's length and width?
   Length 6 cm   Width 3 cm

4. Emma plays netball on a court, which is 31 m long and 15 m wide. To warm up before a game, Emma ran once around the perimeter of the court. How far did Emma run?
   92 m

21

5. Look at the dimensions of the rectangle and find its perimeter.
   12 m

6. Look at the dimensions of the square and find its perimeter.
   12 cm

7. The perimeter of a square is 10 cm. Find the length of each side.
   2.5 cm

8. An ant walks around the edges of a rectangular table top. The table is 2 m long and 1 m wide. How far does the ant walk?
   6 m

Explain to your child that one of the reasons we might measure perimeter would be to estimate the length of a fence or wall we would need to buy or build around an area of land. Encourage your child to first estimate and then measure the perimeter of his or her room at home.

Answers:

22–23 Areas of squares and rectangles
24–25 Areas of compound shapes

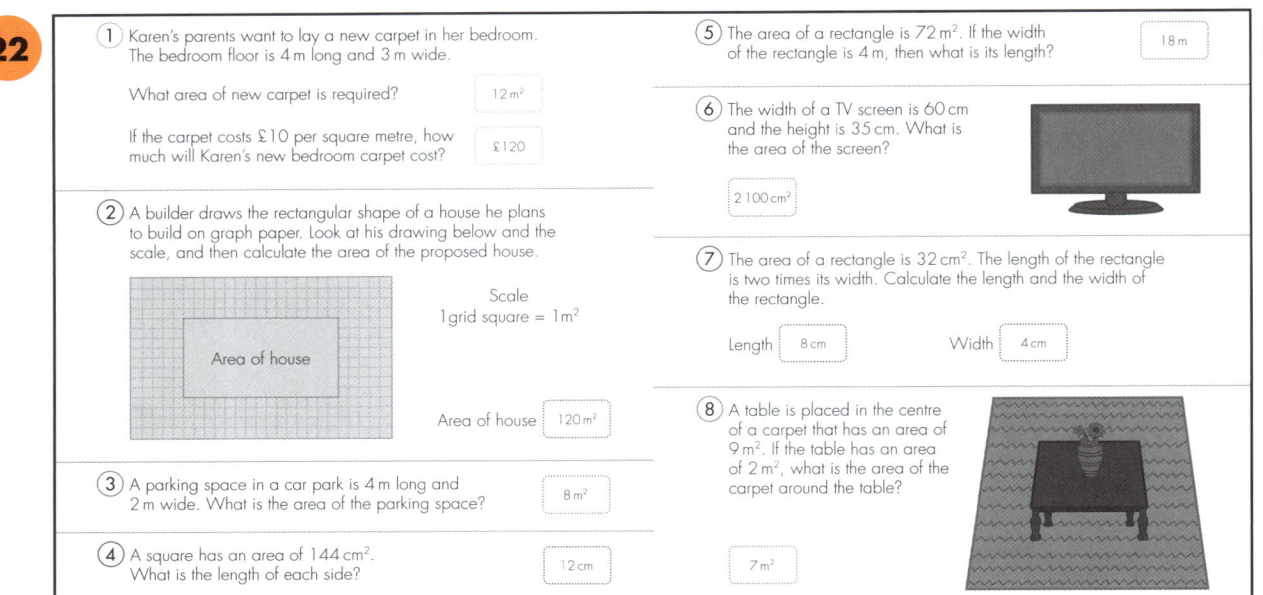

Encourage your child to think of area as the space contained within a shape. Even though the questions on this page involve only the areas of squares and rectangles, broaden your child's understanding of area to cover other shapes such as circles. Point out coins, plates or pizzas as examples of circular areas.

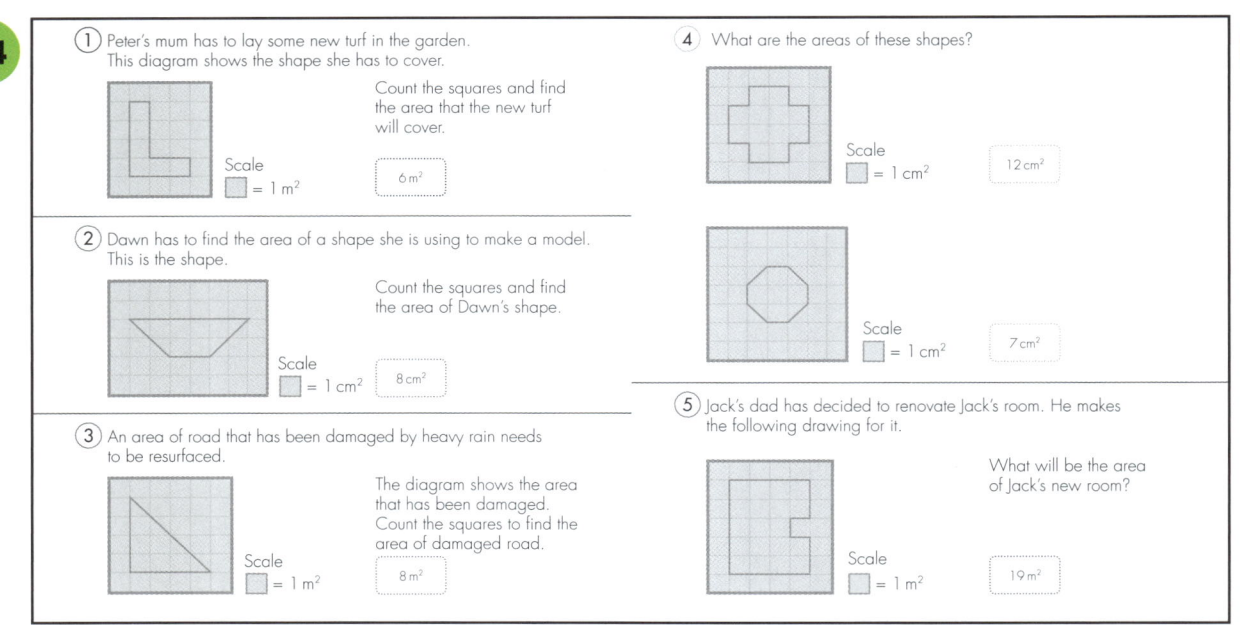

Although most of the compound shapes in these questions are fairly simple, some of the drawings contain halves of squares. Your child must carefully count all of them. Marking on the diagrams whether they are halves or wholes may also be helpful when working out area.

Answers:

26–27 Weights and measures 1
28–29 Weights and measures 2
30–31 Money problems 2, see p.80

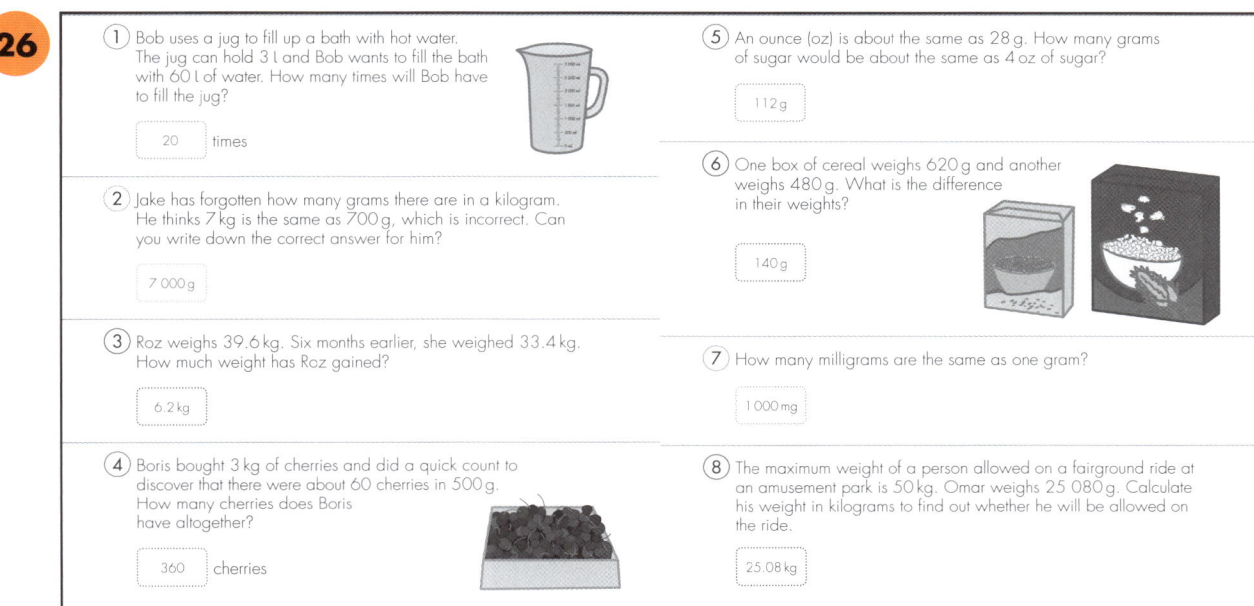

Imagining the scenario described in a problem is the key to solving the problem. If your child finds that difficult, try to relate the problem in some way to items or situations at home.

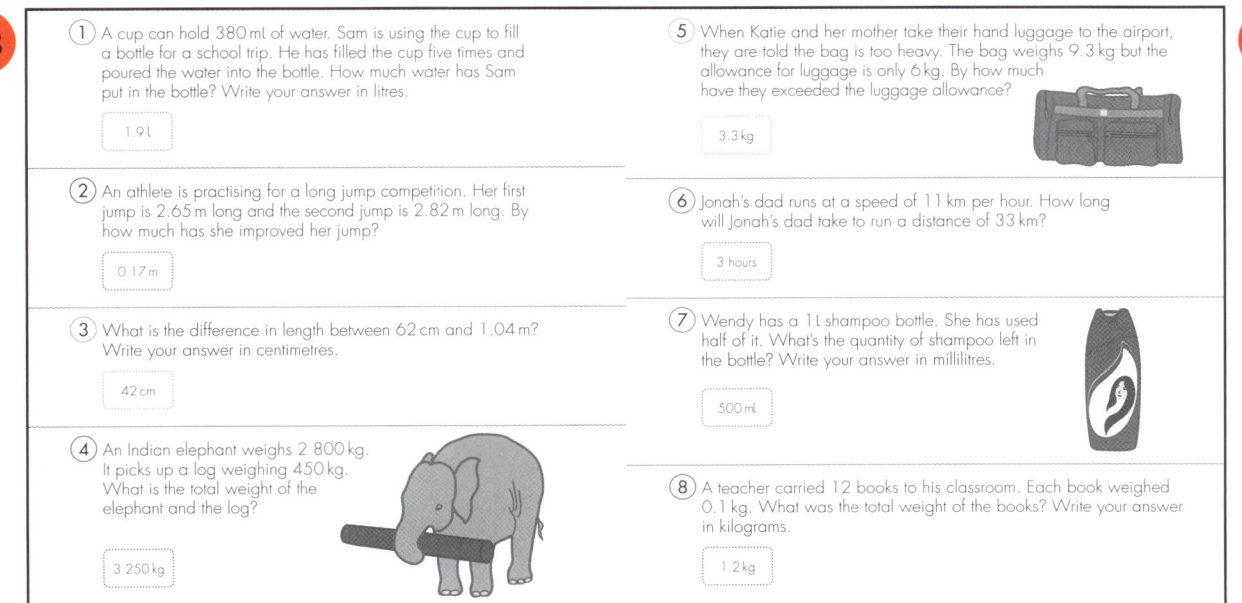

Young children are usually familiar with smaller amounts such as grams and centimetres. Introduce your child slowly to working with larger amounts, such as kilograms and litres, so he or she can gradually build confidence using them.

Answers:

32–33 Decimals 1
34–35 Decimals 2

32

1. A piece of elastic is 0.32 m long. When stretched, the elastic becomes 1.35 m long. By what length has the elastic increased from its original size?
   1.03 m

2. A cook had 1 l of milk in a carton. He used 0.65 l of it while baking a pudding. How much milk is left in the carton?
   0.35 l

3. Add these lengths and write the answer.
   3.12 m + 0.84 m + 0.09 m   **4.05 m**

4. Three boxes are stacked one on top of the other. The first box is 0.16 m high, the second 0.41 m high and the third 0.33 m high. The boxes together need to be 1 m high, but they are not. How much short of 1 m is the stack of boxes?
   0.1 m

33

5. How many millilitres are there in 1.425 l?
   1425 mL

6. Jack, Gina and Grace did some odd jobs for their aunt to earn extra pocket money during their summer holidays. Jack cleaned the garden and earned £2, Gina washed the car and earned £2.10 and Grace painted the fence and earned £1.95. They need £6 for a new set of books they plan to buy together. How much extra money have they made?
   5p

7. Gill buys two large loaves of bread at £2.75 each and one pack of bagels at £1.35. How much change will she get if she pays with a £10 note?
   £3.15

8. A toy brick is 1.8 cm high. If another brick that is 3.4 cm high is placed on top of it, what will be the total height of the two bricks?
   5.2 cm

Your child needs to be able to convert between big and small units, such as kilograms and grams. For example, whenever your child sees 2.3 kg, he or she should immediately be able to convert it to 2 300 g.

34

1. An athlete took part in a local triathlon. She began by running 5.4 km and then swimming 2.7 km. Finally, she cycled to the finishing line. If the total distance of the race was 10 km, how long was the cycle ride?
   1.9 km

2. When two bags of sand are weighed together, they make up 3.65 kg. If one of the bags weighs 1.77 kg, what is the weight of the other bag?
   1.88 kg

3. A cinema ticket costs £10.50 for an adult and £7.20 for a child. If two parents take two children to see a film, what will be the total cost of the tickets?
   £35.40

4. A king cobra is 4.5 m long. If its head and neck region is 0.7 m long, what is the length of the rest of its body?
   3.8 m

35

5. An empty jar weighs 0.60 kg. When filled with sweets, it weighs 1.95 kg. How much do the sweets weigh?
   1.35 kg

6. A bus journey is a distance of 32.4 km. If 16.3 km of the journey has already been covered, how much distance left?
   16.1 km

7. Tim has 1.5 m of train track. Pam has 2.2 m and Sean has 0.5 m. If they join their tracks together, how long will their combined track be?
   4.2 m

8. Four children had a total of £6.50. Together, they spent £3.60 on ice cream. What is the amount of money left?
   £2.90

It is absolutely important that your child positions the decimal point accurately. After your child has finished each question, encourage him or her to double check if the decimal is in the correct place.

Answers:

36–37 Fractions
38–39 Fractions and percentages

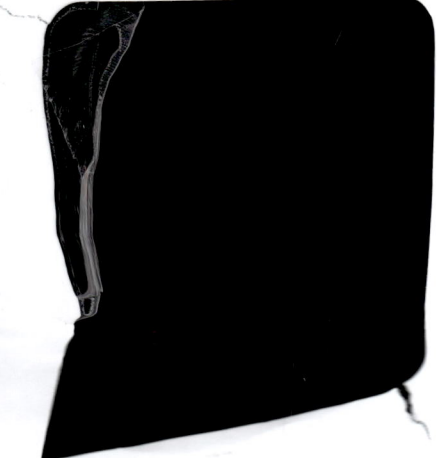

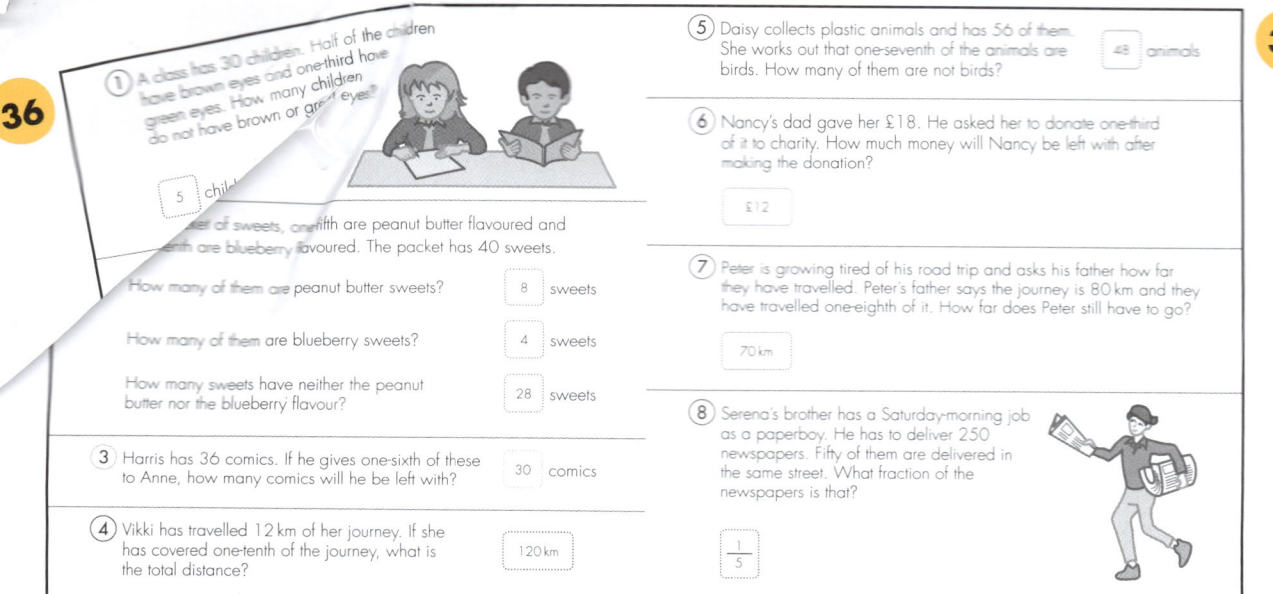

Knowledge of the times tables and the ability to recall them instantly can make it easier for your child to work with fractions and solve multiplication problems quickly.

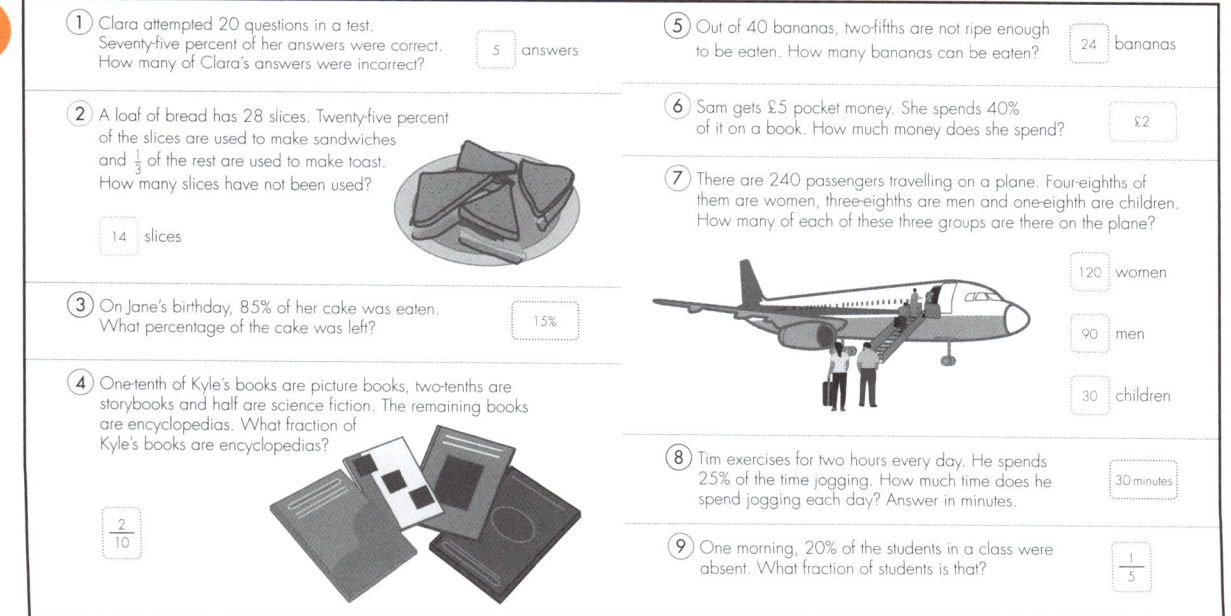

Your child should be able to convert between simple fractions and their percentage equivalents. At this stage, your child should be able to convert $\frac{1}{4}$, $\frac{1}{2}$, $\frac{3}{4}$ and all the tenths into percentages instantly.

Answers:

40–41 Understanding graphs 1
42–43 Understanding graphs 2

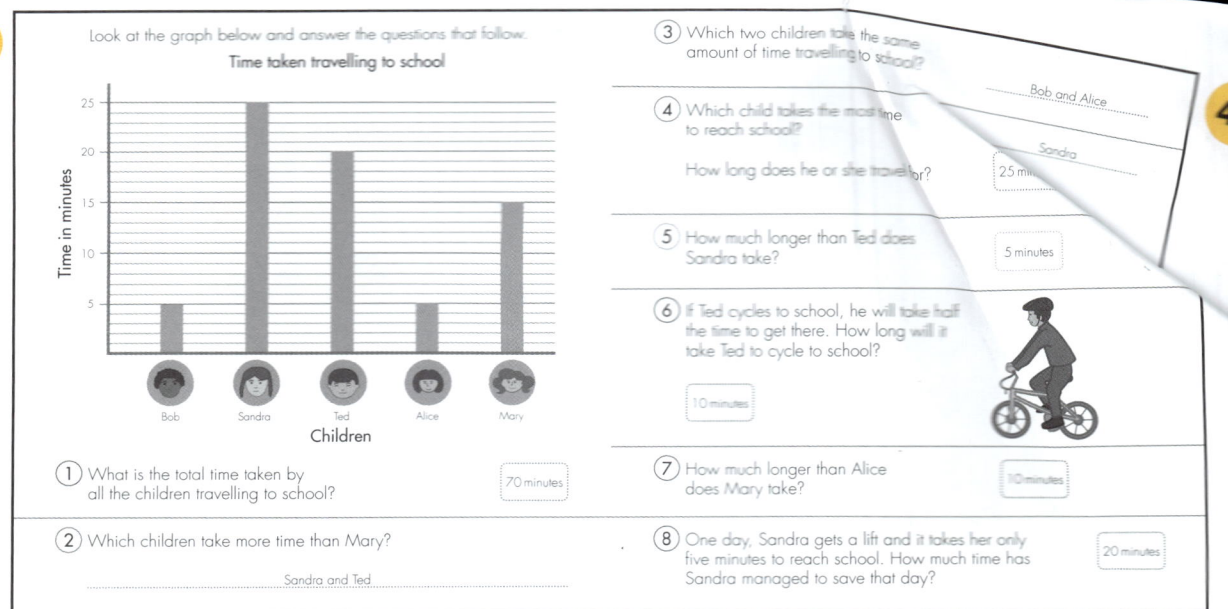

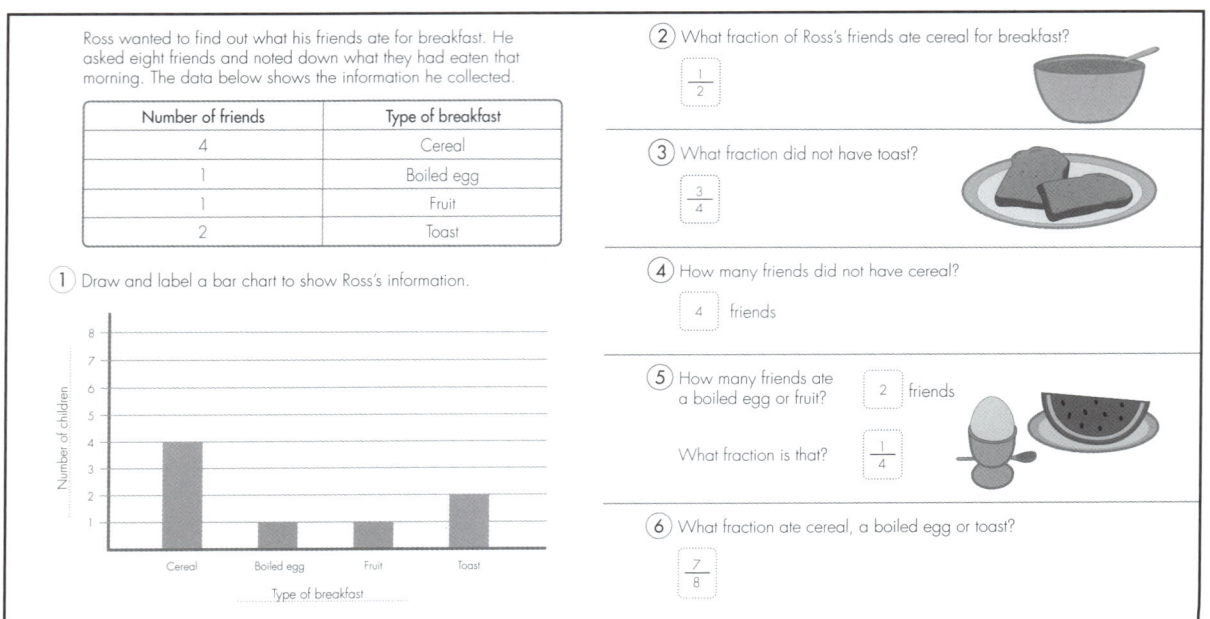

Encourage your child to look at information displays such as match scoreboards or music charts. Ask questions based on the information to see if he or she can read the data correctly.

Encourage your child to make his or her own picture graphs based on data he or she has collected. For example, your child could ask 10 of his or her friends what fruit they like to eat most and then plot the collected data on a graph.

Answers:

44–45 Addition and subtraction 1
46–47 Addition and subtraction 2

44

1. Rashid, Sabah and Michael are saving 1p coins for charity. In six months, Rashid has collected 92 coins, Sabah 85 coins and Michael 103 coins. How much money have they collected in total? Write your answer in pounds.
   £2.80

2. Farmer Frank has put his cattle into barns for winter. He moved 52 cows from one field, 45 cows from another field and 37 cows from a third field. Each barn can hold 40 cows. How many barns did Frank use?
   4 barns

3. A car had 30.95l of petrol in its tank. During a journey, 16.50l of it was used up. How much petrol is left?
   14.45l

4. Three consecutive numbers (numbers in a row) add up to 21. What are the numbers?
   6 7 8

45

5. Two suitcases are put on weighing scales at an airport check-in counter. One suitcase weighs 12.8 kg and the total weight of both of them is 23 kg. How much does the other suitcase weigh?
   10.2 kg

6. One thousand pamphlets were printed for a local museum. Of these, 725 are colour and the rest are black and white. How many black-and-white pamphlets were printed?
   275 pamphlets

7. Jan thinks of a number. She adds 25 to it and then subtracts six. Her final number is 69. What number did Jan start with?
   50

8. When Becky first played a computer game, she scored 478 points. On her second attempt, she scored 680 points. How many more points did Becky score on her second attempt?
   202 points

Addition and subtraction may be taught in different ways, depending on the school. To ensure your child follows a consistent approach, make sure you know what method he or she has been taught.

46

1. When David added three numbers together, he arrived at a total of 68. One of the numbers is 12 and the second number is its double. What is David's third number?
   32

2. Emmie has a collection of 600 CDs. She has decided to give some away to charity. If Emmie gives away 48 CDs, how many will she have left?
   552 CDs

3. Sean wants to give some money to the school fund. He finds 78 p in his wallet and 54 p in his bedroom drawer. He then decides to give £1 of the money to the fund. How much money will Sean keep for himself?
   32 p

4. The total of three numbers is 1 000. If 80 and 250 are two of the numbers, what is the third number?
   670

47

5. In a tin of 90 biscuits, 34 have been broken. How many biscuits are not broken?
   56 biscuits

6. Petra's mum has 86 emails in her inbox, but 49 of them are unwanted spam. How many emails are not spam?
   37 emails

7. Gaia added two numbers together and the sum came to 240. If one of the numbers is 165, what is the other number?
   75

8. Seventy pages of a notebook have been used up. If the notebook has 130 pages, how many blank pages are left?
   60 pages

Your child should have a good working knowledge of addition and subtraction before he or she moves on to learning the times tables and multiplication.

Answers:

48–49 Multiplication and division 1
50–51 Multiplication and division 2
52–53 Money problems 3, see p.80

48

1) In a video game, a player is awarded 15 points every time the frog catches a fly and 20 points when the frog catches a wasp. How many points will a player earn if the frog catches six flies and nine wasps?
270 points

2) Charlie has been saving money to buy his sister a present. He has saved 50p every day for 21 days. How much money has he saved?
£10.50

3) A teacher marked 64 test booklets every evening for six days. How many booklets did the teacher mark in total?
384 booklets

4) Pat went to the gym 132 times in a year. How many times did she go each month?
11 times

49

5) A parcel delivery company has 520 parcels to be delivered by four drivers. How many parcels will each driver need to deliver?
130 parcels

6) Victor thinks of a number that is seven times smaller than 56. Which number did he think of?
8

7) Debbie multiplied a number by itself and got 81 as the product. Which number did Debbie start with?
9

8) A birthday cake is covered with chocolate buttons and cut into eight pieces. Each piece has 6 buttons except one piece, which has 7. How many chocolate buttons were put on the cake?
49 buttons

Knowing the times tables is the key to solving the problems on these pages. Your child should know the tables up to 12 x 12 and be also aware of multiples of 15 and 20.

50

1) A teacher started a maths lesson by writing 10 sums on the board and asking the students to solve them. In the evening, the teacher checked the answers. If the class has 30 children, how many answers did the teacher have to mark?
300 answers

2) Mrs Harris has collected 68 fridge magnets over the years. She decides to buy a smaller fridge, so she distributes the magnets equally between Molly, Isaac, Louis and Isobel. How many fridge magnets does each child receive?
17 magnets

3) A driver collects 10 vouchers every time he spends £1 on petrol. In one week, the driver spent £55 on petrol. If each voucher is worth 2p, how much did the driver earn in vouchers that week?
£11

4) Felt-tip pens come in packets of 20. How many pens will there be in a dozen packets?
240 pens

51

5) Kim divided a number by 12 and arrived at an answer of 15. What number did Kim start with?
180

6) The captain of a ship loaded 600 containers in 12 rows. How many containers are there in each row?
50 containers

7) Ninety sweets are divided among a number of children. If each child receives 15 sweets, how many children are there?
6 children

8) Eighty-four bananas are shared equally among 12 people. How many bananas does each person get?
7 bananas

Your child can sometimes fail to understand the direct relationship between multiplication and division so always encourage him or her to connect the two when working out sums.

Answers:

54–55 Times tables problems 1
56–57 Times tables problems 2

54

1) Billy is 7 years old and Mandy is 12 years old. How many months old are they?

Billy is **84** months old   Mandy is **144** months old

2) A paperboy earns £7 per day.

If he works five days a week, how much will he earn? **£35**

He can earn £12 per day if he works on Saturday and Sunday. How much would he earn in a week if he worked at the weekend, too? **£59**

3) It costs Emmie £12 each time she has a piano lesson. If Emmie has nine lessons, how much will they cost her?

£108

In the Summer term, the cost of each lesson drops. If Emmie has eight lessons then and they cost her £72, how much does each lesson cost?

£9

55

4) For a party, five children collect eight pairs of sunglasses each. How many pairs of sunglasses do they have altogether?

40 pairs of sunglasses

5) How many days are there in nine weeks?

63 days

6) Seven children have collected eight party hats each. What is the total number of hats they have for the party?

56 hats

7) How many months are there in five years?

60 months

8) A teacher has drawn six octagons on the board. How many sides has he drawn in total?

48 sides

The 7 and 8 times tables are often considered to be the most difficult to remember. It is useful to spend time with your child, helping him or her to learn these times tables thoroughly, especially at the higher combinations, such as 6 x 7 and 8 x 9.

56

1) Daniel bought eight boxes of chocolates to take on a holiday. Each box contains 12 chocolates. How many chocolates does Daniel have in total?

96 chocolates

2) William multiplied two by three. He multiplied the answer by four and then doubled it. Finally, he divided that answer by four. Which number did William finish with?

12

3) Adam believes only two single-digit numbers can be multiplied to make 63, but he cannot remember the numbers. Help Adam find out what the two numbers are.

7 and **9**

4) Sarah doubled a number. She then doubled the result and got 32. Which number did Sarah start with?

8

57

5) Which number multiplied by four gives the same answer as six times six?

9

6) The product of which two single-digit numbers gives 35?

7 and **5**

7) Multiply the number of days in a week by the number of months in a year.

84

8) A packet contains eight biscuits. Lorraine wants 48 biscuits to share with her friends. How many packets will she need?

6

When your child is consistently getting his or her times tables correct, concentrate on faster recall. You could generate some more interest by making it competitive using a stop watch.

Answers:

58–59 Ratio problems 1
60–61 Ratio problems 2

58

1. An artist made pink paint by adding one part of red paint to three parts of white paint. If the artist uses 36 parts of white paint, how much red paint will he need?

   12 parts

2. In a class of 24 children, one in every three children is a girl.

   What fraction of the class is boys? **2/3**

   How many girls are there? **8**

3. A car dealer has 50 cars. Out of every 10 cars, two are white and three are red. How many cars of those colours are there?

   15 red cars   **10** white cars

4. For every oak tree in a forest, there are three ash trees. If the forest has 24 oak trees, find the number of ash trees.

   72 ash trees

59

5. A decorator uses eight cans of white paint to every three cans of magnolia paint. If the decorator uses 24 cans of magnolia paint, how many cans of white paint will he use?

   64 cans

6. For every magpie seen in a garden, there are six swallows. If 42 swallows have been seen, how many magpies will have been seen?

   7 magpies

7. Mum gives Clara three times as many cherries as she gives Oliver. If Oliver has eight cherries, how many does Clara have?

   24 cherries

8. John is twice as old as Laura and Laura is twice as old as Sally. If Sally is seven years old, how old is John?

   28 years

Encourage your child to think of ratios as a way of showing the proportions between amounts in a group. For example, 2:3 may be thought of as "for every two parts, there are three other parts".

60

1. Children at a school were asked if they could play a musical instrument. For every three children that could play the guitar, there was one that could play the piano. If there are thirteen pianists at the school, how many guitarists are there?

   39 guitarists

2. For every five boxes of cereal bought, a supermarket hands out a free tub of ice cream. If a man buys 15 boxes of cereal, how many free tubs of ice cream will he receive?

   3 tubs

3. A painter mixed paints in the proportion of five parts white to two parts blue to one part yellow. If he used 20 parts white paint, how many parts blue and yellow did the painter use?

   8 parts blue   **4** parts yellow

4. Bricklayers mix four bags of sand to one bag of cement. If they use eight bags of cement, how many bags of sand will they need?

   32 bags of sand

61

5. The teacher tells the students that three in every eight cats are male. If the students study 24 cats, how many of them should be male and how many female?

   9 male cats   **15** female cats

6. For every yellow clay brick that Maggie has, she has seven blue ones. If Maggie has 56 blue bricks, how many yellow bricks does she have?

   8 yellow bricks

7. The ratio of the weight of Ryan's cat to the weight of Kim's cat is three to four. If Ryan's cat weighs 6 kg, how much does Kim's cat weigh?

   8 kg

8. In a class of 30 children, two out of every three children have brown hair. The rest have blond hair. How many children have brown hair and how many of them have blond hair?

   20 have brown hair   **10** have blond hair

By now, your child should be aware of ratios involving two items, such as 2:3. He or she may have some difficulty with ratio problems involving more than two items. For example, recipes or colour mixes may actually mention ratios such as 1:3:4.

Answers:

62–63 Harder problems 1
64–65 Harder problems 2

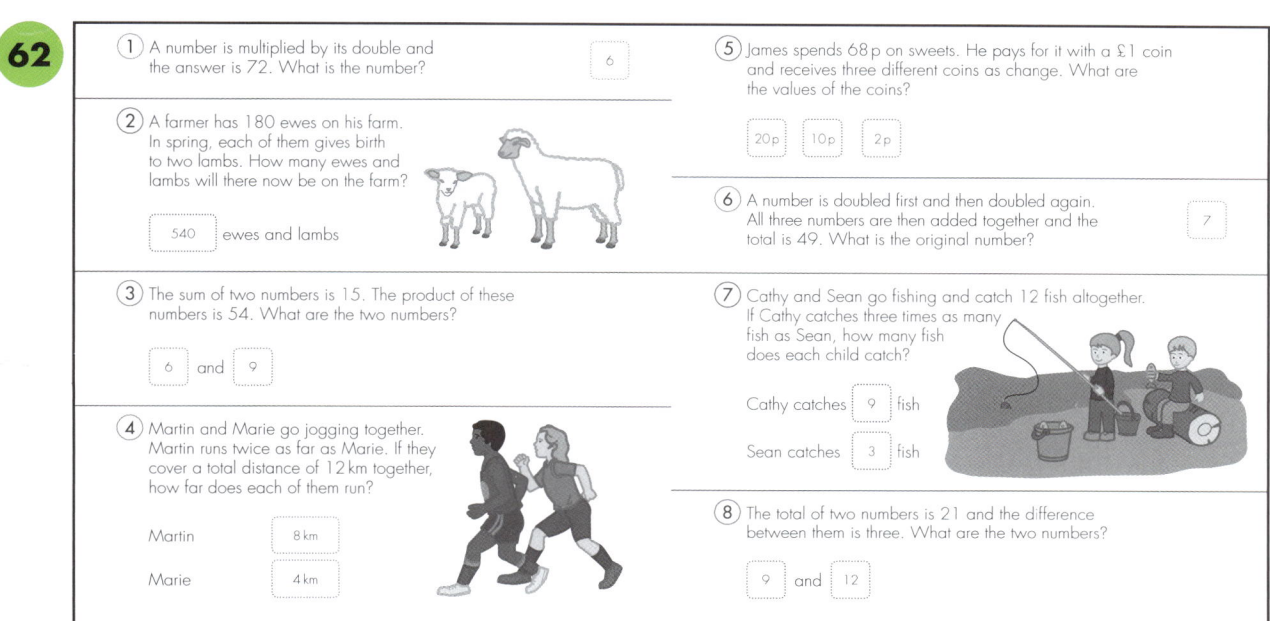

Whatever the problem may be, it is always worth reading the question at least twice. If your child is in a hurry, he or she may miss something important or miss reading one of the numbers needed for the calculation.

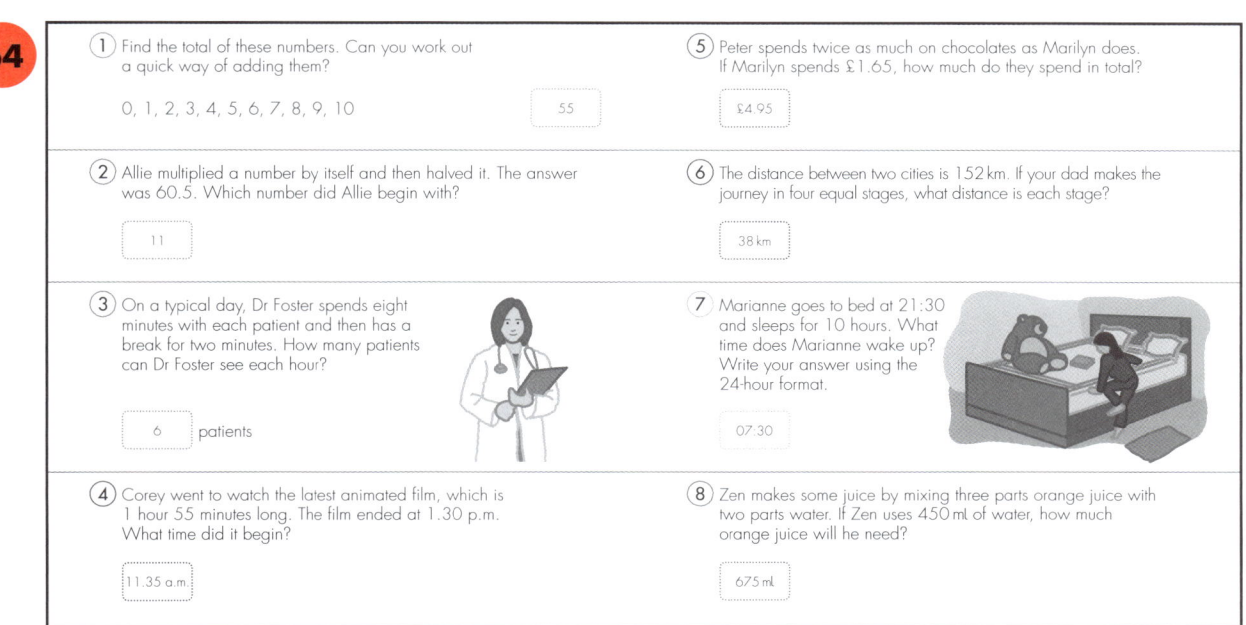

The quick way to add consecutive numbers (0–10) is to multiply the number of consecutive numbers (11) by the middle number (5). Once your child has worked out a problem, encourage him or her to read the question again and make sure the answer makes sense. This is especially true when decimal amounts are involved in a calculation.

Answers:

14–15 Money problems 1
30–31 Money problems 2
52–53 Money problems 3

14

1. Ben's mum uses a £10 voucher to download six books from a website. Each book costs 89p. How much money will she have left after buying the six books? **£4.66**

2. Pam likes to play an online game that costs her 40p per hour. If she plays the game for 29 hours in a month, how much will it cost her? **£11.60**

3. Emmie likes a winter coat she saw at a store for £67.99. She will get a discount of £12.50 if she buys the coat online. How much will the coat cost online? **£55.49**

4. Half of an amount is 85p. How much is the whole amount? **£1.70**

5. A magazine costs £3.50. During a special sale, it was sold at half its price. How much was the magazine sold for? **£1.75**

6. How much is 35p less than £5? **£4.65**

7. A one-way train ticket costs £3.60 and a return ticket for the same journey costs £4.20. If a lady buys two one-way tickets instead of a return ticket, how much extra will the tickets cost her? **£3**

8. Fran and Joseph went to a carnival together. They spent £2 on tickets, £1.60 on balloons, 70p on candy floss and 80p on masks. If they started with a total amount of £10 between them, how much money do they have left? **£4.90**

9. Danny was given £20 for his birthday to treat his friends. Following advice from his mum, Danny saved a quarter of the money for himself. How much money was Danny left with? **£15**

15

These pages test your child's ability to work out problems involving amounts of money. Explain to your child the relationship between pounds and pence and help him or her convert between these units quickly and easily. At this age, your child may have begun to have experience spending pocket money in shops. Stress the importance of knowing the cost of each item being bought, the amount of money handed over and the amount of change he or she should receive.

30

1. Mirka visited a stationery shop. She bought a fancy pencil for £1.50, two marker pens for 80p each and a glue stick for £2.80. How much did Mirka pay in total? **£5.90**

2. Peter receives £5 pocket money each week. Last week, he bought an ice cream for £1.40, lent £2 to his sister and donated 50p to charity. He saved the rest of the money. How much did Peter manage to save? **£1.10**

3. Isobel's class is raising money for charity. Twenty children donated £1 each and nine children donated £1.50 each. How much money has the class raised so far? **£33.50**

4. Rob earns £6.50 an hour. At the end of a day, he earned £39. How many hours did Rob work that day? **6 hours**

5. A shopping bill amounts to £56.28. A quarter of the bill has been spent on fruit. How much money has not been spent on fruit? **£42.21**

6. Kevin bought 2 kg tomatoes, which cost £2.20 per kg. He paid the shopkeeper £10. How much change did the shopkeeper give him? **£5.60**

7. If a pound is worth the same as 1.7 US dollars, what is the value of £5 in US dollars? **Note:** the sign for a dollar is $. **$8.50**

8. A taxi driver charges £2.30 per km. If you travel a distance of 8 km in his taxi, how much will your journey cost? **£18.40**

52

1. Convert these amounts of money from pence to pounds.

   1000p **£10**   700p **£7**
   250p **£2.50**   100p **£1**

2. £4 was shared equally among 5 children. How much money did each child receive? **80p**

3. William and Kate added their money together and then shared it equally among themselves and their son George. If William had £3.50 and Kate had £5.50, how much money did George receive after the money was shared equally among the three of them? **£3**

4. Claire, Bruno, Mark and Ella went for lunch together. They shared the bill of £20.60 equally among themselves. How much money did each of them pay? **£5.15**

53

5. How many £5 notes make up £100? **20 notes**

6. Sarah travels to school by bus. A return ticket costs her £1.30 per day. If Sarah goes to school five days a week, how much does she spend on bus tickets each week? **£6.50**

7. Dan collected £3.60 for charity. His mum said she would give him twice the amount of money he collected.

   How much money will his mum give him? **£7.20**

   How much money would Dan have collected in total? **£10.80**

8. David got £200 as a birthday present. He bought himself two new computer games that cost £49.99 each.

   How much did the two games cost in total? **£99.98**

   How much money does David have left after buying the two games? **£100.02**